The Road of Souls

The Road of Souls
Reflections on the Mississippi

by Nick Lichter

edited by Margaret Wallace Lichter

FIRST EDITION, 2nd printing

WING DAM PRESS

Ferryville, WI

The Road of Souls
Reflections on the Mississippi
by Nick Lichter

Edited by Margaret Wallace Lichter
Book design by Mikaele Witt

ISBN: 0-9758615-0-6
Library of Congress Control Number: 2004094517

This book includes selections from a play by Tennessee Williams,
from Camino Real, copyright © As "Camino Real," revised and published version, ©1953
The University of the South Renewed 1981 The University of the South.
Reprinted by permission of New Directions Publishing Corp.

The author made a good faith effort to ensure the accuracy
and completeness of information contained in this book.
Any errors, omissions or derogatory impressions of the people,
places or events portrayed herein are unintentional.

For Margaret

Acknowledgements

About a week downstream from the headwaters there was a sign at the river's edge offering drinking water. There was a picnic table too, and a convenient place to land. On the picnic table was a coffee can and inside it a spiral pad knotted with kite string to a little butt of pencil. People headed downriver had written their names, addresses, destinations and departure dates. Everything's downriver at that point, all one-way.

The list suggests maybe three of four people look toward New Orleans from Itasca in a year. Some years it floods and no-one goes.

It takes a long time. It takes luck too. What's needed most is help. Lots of little bits of help, here and there. And once in a while big chunks of help, at certain times, in certain places. So I've been making a spiral pad list of helpers. By now it is a very long list. I check it once in a while. I try to remember. If I get a chance I'll stop by when I'm in town and say "Hi".

We made it. Here it is. Thank you. Thanks a lot. I hope you enjoy our story.

"It is I who travel in the winds
It is I who whisper in the breeze
I shake the trees
I shake the earth
I trouble the waters on every land."

—Kah-Ge-Ga-Gah-Bowh, 1847

Contents

Introduction

My canoe was an honest chair, responding and obedient to the work of my hands. For months on end I reached a paddle's blade into the river gripping the pommel close by my heart. Dip and pull, dip and pull. It was honest work, heart's work, monotonous as a metronome and spellbinding in its simplicity. Slowly, very slowly, the river unfurled like a shimmering liquid ribbon through a widening corridor of trees. Each day I would go where it led, centering in the current. Then, at night as I made camp I would watch it withdraw into the darkness, unrelenting, mysterious, disappearing away before my eyes.

This book is also the work of my hands. But I am not so honest here as in my canoe. My direction is not so faultless as the river's. These inky, jotted characters, channels of words, are numerous as paddlestrokes. But they are only shadows, the shadings of a pen. They do not move. They are not like the outward spreading rings of the paddlestrokes that tolled my passage downriver.

On May 6, 1991, Mike Cichanowski from We-No-Nah Canoe, Inc. of Winona, Minnesota loaned me a seventeen-foot, flatwater, marathon canoe. His receipt read, "To be used on Mississippi River Trip leaving May 18th to October??" I'd already assembled other gear. Over the next few days I hinged a deck lid and a bulkhead forward in the canoe to prevent my gear from rain and theft. In the rear I fitted a bicycle mount. With the front tire removed, my bike nested there perfectly.

Aft of the decking I riveted in a seat and a portage bar, forming a cockpit. Over the course of the voyage that compartment proved to be an efficient space. By journey's end it had been my chart room, library, infirmary, exercise room, wardrobe, laundry, pantry, prayer cubicle, observation deck, lounge, kitchen, and water closet. It also became my sweat lodge. For aesthetics I painted an eagle's head either side of the bow, a thunderbird on the deck lid, and on the floor, a heart.

"Oh I am a cook and a captain bold,
And the mate of this canoe;
And a bosun tight and a midshipmite,
And the crew and pilot too."

Captain Willard Glazier, an early Mississippi canoeist, wrote that bit of doggerel in 1887, describing himself. It characterized me pretty well, too. Unbidden, the rhyme would crop up and play in my thoughts, attracted there by paddling. Paddling is a canoeist's stride, as individual as one's walking gait. Though the sequence of paddling is both ancient and universal, each person's rhythm is unique. Dip, pull, lift and reach, was the simplest sequence fitted and timed within others. Three strokes starboard and three strokes port tracked my canoe straight down the current. The river's current threaded days and nights in succession until I'd spent a season. The seasons fit within years, and years within lifetimes. Somehow a sequence of lifetimes, before Glazier's and beyond my own, fits the Mississippi. When I companioned the river on its journey I lived within its cadence. For one summer, my days and paddlestrokes, even the beats of my heart were in concordance with the Mississippi.

So many things are different now. If only my desk had an honest chair. If only I could grip my pen with two hands to write. With one hand held close by my heart and the other reaching perhaps I could write for you the river's story. I would track and alternate perfectly as the river's current, past and present, thoughts and events, war and peace, the body and flow of this great country. But no, the river has too much power. It is too wide and too long. Too many people have watched from its bank as day and night come and go, and spring and winter, and birth and death. With two strong hands I still could not write the river's story. Nor even with my heart.

The river reconciles time and presence in its unceasing flow. With the river I saw northern Minnesota's ice in May and its cold rains. We stayed on together to meet chirping cicadas in the Louisiana bayous of southern August. With the river I canoed through the present, hearing people now, but also hearing the past. I heard words deeper than time alone can make them, words of place, river tones. Native Americans, the first people of the river, sing the deepest tones. Their voices move, and are joined on many levels, even by our own. Set to the river's rhythm and layered upon one another those chords become a song longer than the river's thousands of miles. This book is only a few bars of that deep, long, beautiful song. It is my transcription of one summer's chant.

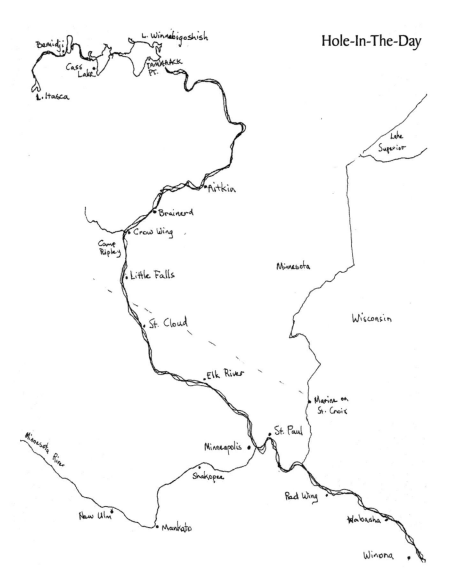

Hole-In-The-Day

Bemidji

L. Winnebigoshish

Cass Lake

TAMARACK PT.

L. Itasca

Lake Superior

Aitkin

Brainerd

Crow Wing

Camp Ripley

Minnesota

Little Falls

Wisconsin

St. Cloud

Elk River

Marine on St. Croix

St. Paul

Minnesota River

Minneapolis

Shakopee

Red Wing

New Ulm

Mankato

Wabasha

Winona

Hole-In-The-Day

There is no beginning to a Mississippi river trip. The journey just evolves. One reads Huck Finn, spends years wistfully remembering childhood freedom, dreams away a decade or two and then, one day, it happens.

On May 16, 1991 I left for Lake Itasca, Minnesota. Friends had agreed to care for my house and dog and to forward my mail. The first night out I stayed in Minneapolis, with college friends. They helped me shop for last-minute items: sunscreen, mosquito netting, a lifevest and a Minnesota fishing license. The next morning we parted ways at the Interstate, they to a Twins game, I bound for the headwaters. We waved to each other as I looped through a long sweeping exit ramp, up and away, cloverleafing into the west.

I was besieged by more than a few doubts about the logic of my undertaking. Was I about to dive into a very wet mid-life crisis? If I succeeded in paddling all the way to New Orleans, so what? I had just been laid-off from a job of ten years. Was my river journey just an escape? Was I just running away?

Outside of Spirit Lake, Minnesota twenty miles from the river's source at Lake Itasca, there is a thirty foot high plastic statue of St. Urho. The townspeople had just erected the saint's likeness in honor of their Scandinavian heritage. Urho, depicted in monkish habit, holds aloft a pitchfork with a giant grasshopper impaled feet skyward on the tangs. Urho once banished a plague of grasshoppers from Finland with the simple words, "Grasshoppers, Grasshoppers, Go away!" It was an odd monument by my lights, the first of many. Yet it was also a good harbinger promising an interesting journey. And the saint's words were effective. My doubts dispersed and I drove on to Lake Itasca.

The year 1991 was the hundredth anniversary of the park. I spent most of my first day there bicycling round the lake, spinning down roads that wove through pines massive as the sky. The trees, centuries old, commune with more than rustling of branches and needles. They exude a fragrance of brotherhood, their stature is dignity, and their symmetry is earth's most perfect conduit to the heavens. Minnesota's tallest and oldest white pine is at Itasca. It marries the earth and sky, presiding amongst others of its specie, drawing identity from them. Not far away a red pine, likewise tallest and oldest, spires within a community of its peers. These largest trees give strength and beauty to all that surrounds them. Looking upwards I noticed in the topmost scantling of the red pine's crown that a pileated woodpecker had made a rectangular hole.

Early park history has at least one colorful defense of this rare first growth timber. Lumber barons must have been especially insatiable and belligerent. Mary Gibbs, park superintendent in 1903, was threatened to be shot after ordering the Mississippi-Schoolcraft Boom and Improvement Company to open its dam on the lake. The company wanted to dam water high enough to float logs down the little stream that becomes the Mississippi. Mary Gibbs wanted it low enough to keep the park trees from drowning. Thanks to her courageous defense, these oldest and largest pines still spire above Itasca's southern shore.

Close beneath the pines I found a stone monument, unmarked, almost hidden. It bore this plaque, "Reverend Joseph A. Gilfillan preached the first sermon at the source of the Mississippi river in May 1881 on the knoll approximately 200 feet northwesterly of this tablet. The text was 'Then had thy peace been as a river'." Reverend Gilfillan and his company had covered sixty miles of wilderness from White Earth, Minnesota to conduct the ceremony. The complete text is found in an Old Testament passage from Isaiah, 48:14. "O that thou hadst hearkened to my commandments! Then had thy peace been as a river, and thy righteousness as the waves of the sea." Gilfillan was active on the upper river in an era that was anything but peaceful.

Just down the road from the monument, a fire watchtower offers visitors a commanding view of the surrounding woodlands. The park is at the crux of several continental divides. Looking out from the watchtower in any direction one can see into the distance so far that green woodlands turn blue and become sky. It is a view as from the top of a high mountain, or that of a bird perched in Itasca's tallest trees. I remember descending the tower's steps that evening, seeing birds' nests and spiders' webs built in odd corners of the framework. The watchtower's steel ribs rattled in the wind and their evening shadow lay eastward over the pines like a long skeleton of man. It came to me then that the quote on the stone monument would guide me down the Mississippi. As I canoed from Itasca to the sea I reaffirmed that association many times.

The word "peace" as used by Reverend Gilfillan back in 1881, is translated in some modern bibles as prosperity. Prosperity is substantial stuff, able to meet hunger and quench thirst. Peace is its own prosperity. It is both the source and the flowing into emptiness. The source of the Mississippi is that place of highest emptiness: a hole in the dome of the sky, the back of a bird in Minnesota's tallest pine, a spider's web in the watchtower, or a rock at Lake Itasca's edge. I choose Gilfillan's rock, a great red stone, a solid heart. It is the source that still resonates within when I listen for it carefully. It is the flow of the river, the rhythm of a paddle, the beat of my own heart. In my most tranquil center I kept Gilfillan's message and followed it through countless joinings until it became part of the unknowable. That rock and the idea of peace, like the source of the river, begins and ends in the infinite, in the breath of the Great Mysterious.

Late that evening I prepared a meal which became my standard voyage fare: rice and carrots flavored with boullion. Things were perking along at a pretty boil when I noticed a small flame coming from the stove's vented fuel cap. The only proper flame is from the stove's burner. I tried to extinguish the cap but it relit, several times. Then suddenly the cap's flame got much bigger, even bigger than the burner's flame. In a matter of seconds the stove was torching upwards in a dangerous jet. I put on a glove, grabbed the stove and threw it into the lake. My doubts returned.

With darkness raccoons began rummaging the campground in force. Their curious clicking noises roused me from an unsettled sleep. I left my tent and cleared the picnic table of food and gear. Out over the lake a sickle moon held a bright star in its cradle. Both the star and moon were reflected in broken pieces all across the dark water. The night's breeze was raising a chop, just enough to keep the lake alive. The night itself, in tiniest of little moments, was draining off, down the river on a long, long journey to the sea. The whole universe seemed to have assembled, awaiting places in a procession, a watery mosaic quietly filing downstream. The procession had begun incomparably long ago. And had been incomparably repeated. I thought then how extraordinary it was that my turn was at hand.

The Mississippi north from Iowa and Wisconsin to its source at Lake Itasca, Minnesota reflects the dawning of America. Names of Dakota, Winnebago, Ojibwa, Sac and Fox chiefs and early pioneers are preserved in the towns and cities, counties, streams, bluffs and parks of the upper Mississippi. In the early days the native names were like pulsars of the north country, shining constellations in the hard winter's night sky. They were names of tribal dynasties, luminaries that guided their people in safe passage through time. The dynastic forebears of Minnesota predated the American Revolution and held steady through the War of 1812 and later, Black Hawk's War. But with each battle of each war an encroaching eastern glow intensified. It kept moving further west and further north, feeding upon primitive villages, a photogen of the Industrial Age. By the Civil War it had reached the upper Mississippi. Then that glowing animus found the tribal dynasties and broke over them irresistible as morning's light. Like stars at dawn the dynasties were extinguished and disappeared.

The Mississippi of the north seems little more than a watery footpath. My first days on the river I sometimes couldn't turn the canoe tight enough to avoid hitting its curving banks. The river demanded that I go more slowly, that I be less forceful, that I cease trying to impose my own direction. Though very small, the river was insistent and already powerful. In the marshy flats where my eye could see no passage the river beckoned from beneath the surface. There its expressive features, its deeper face, spoke simply and quietly. Wild celery leaned with the current, beckoning me to follow where it pointed. The river's banks were lined with tall thin stalks of last year's wild rice. Delicate as a woman's hair the brown grasses dallied with the wind. Spring's aroma hinted from the green shoots rising at their base. Gently the river drew me along its way.

For a season I was the river's companion. I wanted its peace as my own. I wanted to learn the river's channels and its life. To me the most interesting story centered on America's Western Expansion. The river represented the edge of the frontier then, at least for European people. For First Americans I am not sure what the river represented. In my mind their native story is the river's most compelling, perhaps because it is almost inaccessible now. Learning their story was very much like canoeing the Mississippi. By turns it was slow, beautiful, painful and always a source of awe. It is as though people, both living and dead, have been assigned to wait at places on the river bank to tell a certain story, a piece of a story really, to any passersby who will listen. Many, very many, of the storytellers are native. Out of respect, or perhaps in humble acknowledgment, the river wears that living index of their names as its own.

The story that follows is another source of the Mississippi. It is the story of Hole-in-the-Day, an Indian chief of the Ojibwa. It is also the story of Ta-o-ya-te-du-ta, Little Crow, a Dakota chief. It is a story begun long ago, when flames of the Civil War were engulfing all of America. Minnesota's native tribes, patient beacons throughout the ages, could not withstand its firestorm. Young braves watched entranced as settlers drained from the northwoods, south to the crucible of war. They watched farmers made soldiers march endlessly into the giant open maw. In the white heat of war's doom legions immolated spontaneously. Hoping to reforge the legends of their ancestors, young braves thrust their own people into that war's furnace. They fanned into being the Minnesota Conflicts of 1862. One conflict involved the Ojibwa and another, more famous, the Dakota.

Old, elemental similarities, more profound than the Conflicts, minded those early people of the upper river. Both tribes have a tradition of life after death. For the Ojibwa it is like this:

The soul is supposed to stand immediately after the death of the body, on a deep beaten path, which leads westward; the first object he comes to in following this path, is the great Oda-e-min (Heartberry), or strawberry, which stands on the roadside like a huge rock, and from which he takes a handful and eats on his way. He travels on till he reaches a deep rapid stream of water, over which lies the much dreaded Ko-go-gaup-o-gun or rolling and sinking bridge; once safely over this as the traveller looks back it assumes the shape of a huge serpent swimming, twisting and untwisting its folds across the stream...the soul arrives in the land of spirits, where he finds his relatives accumulated since mankind was first created; all is rejoicing, singing and dancing; they live in a beautiful country...It is that kind of paradise which he only by his manner of life on this earth is fitted to enjoy...The Ojibway believes his home after death to lie westward. In their religious phraseology, the road of souls is sometimes called Ke-wa-kun-ah, "Homeward road." It is, however, oftener named Che-ba-kun-ah (road of souls). In the ceremony of addressing their dead before depositing them in the grave, I have often heard the old men use the word Ke-go-way-se-kah (you are going homeward).[1]

While the journey is different for the Dakota, there are some important commonalities.

To the human body the Dakota give four spirits. The first is supposed to be a spirit of the body and dies with the body. The second is a spirit which always stays with or near the body. Another is the soul which accounts for the deeds of the body and is supposed by some to go south, by others west after the death of the body. The fourth always lingers with the small bundle of hair of the deceased, kept by the relations until they have a chance to take it into the enemy's country, where it becomes a roving restless spirit, bringing death and disease...they believe that the true soul that goes south or west is immortal.[2]

For both tribes the deceased's immortal soul travels after death. Other people, or other parts of the spirit, are left behind to continue battles, strife and contention. But the immortal soul leaves. It goes with the sun to where the day is finished, to the south, or west. It goes to the place of peace.

The selection quoted above, "The Religion of the Dakotas," was found unfinished among James Lynd's effects after he was killed during the Dakota Conflict. His death points up a topical similarity between Dakota and Ojibwa in those days. Both tribes had serious problems with certain traders. Lynd was a trader and employee of Nathan Myrick. Lynd notoriously debauched Dakota women and corrupted braves with alcohol. So did Joseph R. Brown, the Dakota's appointed government agent. Brown perpetrated further evil when he failed to plant Dakota communal fields in 1861. A political appointee, Brown was displaced after Lincoln's election. He left the agency in spring without sowing food crops as specified by treaty agreements. The result was starvation for Dakotas during the winter of 1861 and into the summer of 1862.

In the north, during that same period, Hole-in-the-Day's Ojibwas were also disquieted. Natives of mixed blood, half-breeds, had each been assigned 80 acres of land in the Treaty of 1855. Since they held clear title they were free to dispose of land as they pleased. It was worthless as farmland, so many sold their acreage at very low prices to lumber interests. The tracts probably sold for $20 or less. A few years later, when lumber boomed, the Ojibwa had been completely disenfranchised. Discontent escalated with the Civil War. Though the Ojibwa had virtually no stake in the war's outcome, braves were pressed into service by traders anxious to fill the state's draft quotas. They 'enlisted' Ojibwas after discussions liberally supplied with whiskey. Also during the war, treaty payments were delayed by specie shortage. Finally, in the weeks just before the U.S.-Ojibwa Conflict, a white mob hung two Ojibwa boys. The boys had gotten drunk on trader whiskey and thrown stones at a passing German peddler. One of the stones killed him. They were hung without trial, enraging the Ojibwas and their chief, Hole-in-the-Day.

Chief Hole-in-the-Day was born during an eclipse in 1800. That's how he got his name. The Ojibwa, a tribe also known as the Chippewa, today call themselves the Anishanabe. A literal translation of their word for eclipse is "fissure in the sky through which light streams," i.e. a hole in the sky, or hole in the day. In the Ojibwa's view light came from outside the sky's dome. Their source of light was so pervasive and encompassing that a mere trickle, only that which streamed through a hole in the dome, provided daylight for the entire earth. Suddenly, in comparison, our modern concept of sun becomes very small. Our world view limits the sun, holds it to be never more capable of brightening the dome than in the past. Understanding light as did the Ojibwa expands it to infinite, cosmic proportions. Man cannot know or comprehend the immensity of the sun. In their view daylight poured into emptiness, channeling through an aperture. Light entered the dome and became a flow of illumination and warmth. That ancient aperture, the hole-in-the-day, is still a place on the river. It can still be a place of origin. The Ojibwa's hole-in-the-day marks an archaic point of entry, the fragile openess to an older world. It is an openness that has been gradually closing, first darkened by western expansion and now almost completely eclipsed by our modern scientific minds.

Chief Hole-in-the-Day was the first of a dynasty. He is most famous for expanding Ojibwa lands into northern Minnesota, traditionally Dakota territory. In treaties with the U.S. at Prairie du Chien, Wisconsin in 1825, Hole-in-the-Day and his father, Chief Curly Head, claimed Dakota lands for the Ojibwa. Though acknowledging Dakota hereditary rights, they claimed the territory by conquest. They argued that all U.S. territorial claims were based on conquest and therefore the tribe's Minnesota claim, by the same right of conquest, was equally valid. The U.S. negotiators found the argument convincing and honored the Ojibwa's claim.

In that Treaty of 1825 native lands of Minnesota were bounded by a line that started just north of Minneapolis at Marine on St. Croix and ran northwest, generally parallel to the Mississippi. It crossed the river a bit north of present-day St. Cloud. The northern terminus was called "Peace Rock," near the Watab fur trading post. The Ojibwa were to have lands north of the line and the Dakota south of it. Lands adjacent to the line were to be shared in common for purposes of hunting and traffic, a buffer zone. But in those days rivers were the main arteries of communication and trade. Instead of a buffer zone, the Mississippi corridor became a no man's land. It hosted a blood feud between Dakota and Ojibwa that lasted until the middle of the century.

Minneapolis, located proximate to several rivers—the Mississippi, St. Croix, Minnesota, Crow, Rum and Elk—grew as a hub fed by those arteries. Tribes drawn to Minneapolis for trade frequently collided in incredible violence. Whether by chance meeting, or deliberate ambush, the outcome was often bloodshed. Dakota and Ojibwa killed one another and danced scalps in the very midst of the frontier city. Elk River, forty miles north, was the scene of several reciprocated massacres. There were others at Lake Harriet, Stillwater, St. Anthony, and on the St. Croix and Rum Rivers. Both Hole-in-the-Day and his son were active participants in these bloodlettings, literally to the grave. In one incident, Dakotas defiled Hole-in-the-Day's grave. In retaliation his son and followers ambushed the raiders, killing ten of them. Six scalps and a victim's decapitated head were carried back for display at the village trading post in Crow Wing.

Hole-in-the-Day was formally recognized as chief by U.S. officials to acknowledge his bravery against the British during the War of 1812. Later, he was elected war chief by Bear Clan Ojibwas in 1825, but he was never considered a hereditary chief. He had no ancestral title to pass but his name. His son Que-we-sans, The Boy, or Bad Boy, took the name Hole-in-the-Day upon his father's death. Through force of character and matrilineal inheritance he, too, became chief. He attracted followers among traditional clans and formed his own band at Gull Lake near the Crow Wing trading post. He was known for brave and impetuous behavior. Though his authority was recognized, he was not always well liked, particularly by other chiefs. In 1847 he negotiated cession of tribal lands in the Treaty of Fond-du-Lac. Older chiefs, jealous of Hole-in-the-Day, had tried to begin council negotiations without him. But Henry Rice, representing the government, insisted on waiting. When negotiations ended, treaty terms provided Hole-in-the-Day with personal land holdings and his authority was recognized by all, not least by himself. In his words, "The land you want belongs to me. I am a greater chief than my father; through my mother I am hereditary chief of the Chippewa nation. If I say 'sell', our great father will have it. If I say not, he will go without it. These Indians that you see have nothing to say about it. I approve of the treaty and consent to same."[3]

The Government used those lands purchased from Hole-in-the-Day to bring yet another tribe into Minnesota's disputed territory, the Winnebago. This tribe was removed from Wisconsin in the mid 1830's following the Black Hawk War, partly as punishment, but mostly to open Wisconsin lands for settlers. They were positioned west of the Mississippi near Long Prairie, Minnesota to act as buffer between the Dakota and Ojibwa. In reality their population only increased the number of combatants in the area. Incidents and violence continued. Ironically, the government determined to solve this problem by adding yet more combatants. A military outpost was established on the Mississippi at Fort Ripley, just south of Gull Lake and present day Brainerd, Minnesota. Located near Hole-in-the-Day's village, the Fort was supposed to stabilize relations between tribes and guard the trade agency across the river at Crow Wing. By 1855 increased tribal bloodshed and settler's pressure for new lands had grown so great the Winnebago were repositioned again. This time the government put them on lands purchased from Little Crow's Dakota, on hand for the U.S.-Dakota Conflict.

Hole-in-the-Day's people, the Ojibwa, still own sizeable landholdings near the Mississippi headwaters. Paddling from the river's source takes one through the center of Ojibwa lands. I first entered the Ojibwa reservation at its furthest upstream edge. The Mississippi sinuates through a narrow butt of land there connecting Lake Andrusia with Cass Lake. The banks are so low I could overlook from one lake to the other. Rip-rap of quarried limestone lines the bends, impeding erosion. A local surveyor told me the improvements had been undertaken to preserve embedded human bones from washing into the river. The Ojibwa have buried their dead on this river-cut isthmus for centuries. In legend, their ancestors fought many battles on this scrap of land. Now the river has all but washed it away. Native burial lodges clustered on its southern end overlook a bay of Lake Andrusia. The long, low wooden burial vaults have peaked roofs and a little hole at one end, hardly sized for a bird. While I paddled toward the isthmus, fluff from cottonwood trees floated soft as a requiem onto the lake surface. It settled round my canoe like little clouds, the stuff of tree flowers, a rain of spirits.

I had breakfast in the village of Cass Lake. The area is known to tourists as Paul Bunyan country, perhaps in larger-than-life countermyth to Chief Hole-in-the-Day. Modern Ojibwa still sell timber from reservation lands to the logging industry. Minnesota's cafes with their cinnamon rolls and black coffee are still home to tall tales of timber cuts, and snow melts and, that day, of fish stories. When I was there both local papers, the *Cass Lake Times* and the *Ojibwe News*, were running articles dealing with fishing season's opening day. Fishing is more than a sport in Minnesota, it is a passion, a ritual and an industry. "The Opener" is spring's payoff for having endured winter. It is public confirmation that the big freeze is over, that glaciation and the Ice Age are forestalled another year. When the Great Mysterious exhales new earth's warm breath of spring in Minnesota, it's time to go fishing.

Both papers also carried articles about Eurasian Milfoil. The Minnesota Department of Natural Resources (MDNR) posts warnings at boat landings that this exotic transplant can ruin Minnesota's lakes. Eurasian Milfoil is a home aquarium plant that began infecting Lake Minnetonka in 1987. By 1990 it had spread to 32 other lakes. People in the "Land of Ten Thousand Lakes" take water plants very seriously, just as they take fishing seriously. But other than articles about Milfoil and fishing, the two papers in Cass Lake have little in common.

The *Ojibwe News* is primarily a native paper. All of page nine was a Miller Brewing ad listing 1991's remaining national pow wow schedule. Front page in the *Ojibwe News* was an obituary of Chief Art Gahbow written by R. J. LaFromboise, former president of the National Tribal Chairman's Association. He used the obituary to warn present tribal leadership against jealousy, calling it "the big J." He charted progress during Gahbow's reign, "...the last twenty years of Indian movement from stoicism, Indian activism, to bingoism." Two pages later I read a column entitled, "Reflections from Anishanabe Ojibwe Country," by Francis Blake, Jr. (Wub-e-ke-niew). His column was also a bit out of range for my understanding, though in a more disturbing way.

> Crooked English has many words and many definitions. It's slick and slippery. The names change, the definitions change—but the same thieving thought is here, there, and the underlying structure hasn't changed for centuries.

When Moses was on his way down from the Mountain, he dropped at least one Stone Tablet and broke it. 'Thou Shalt Not Lie;' 'Thou Shalt Not be Greedy;' 'Thou Shalt Live in Harmony With Creation;' 'Thou Shalt Not Foul and Pollute Anybody's Nest;' and 'Thou Shalt Respect All of Creation' never made it down the mountain. What goes around comes around, and what turns, returns. It's our turn to study the Indo-Europeans, his value system and religion, and what his sickness of greed, violence and linear dishonesty have done to this world. Civilization has to return to this continent again.

A further two pages on, the "Ask Grandma" advice column was masted by a rocking chair. This piece at least was intelligible,

Ni Mishomis...told me to tell you, "never mind, those people are like a dog running in circles and chewing its own tail. Eventually its tail is gone and then it'll bite its own hind end. That's how strange they are and why they got away with so much already." That's the difference between us and them, and they don't get to have it all. We still have our tails to fluff and we're a long way from our own hind ends...

The *Ojibwe News* preserves the legacy and contentious spirit of Chief Hole-in-the-Day. But Grandma's imagery, a dog chasing itself, hearkens back to Little Crow. On the night the Sioux Conflict of 1862 began he said: "You are like dogs in the Hot Moon when they run mad and snap at their own shadows." The dog running in circles is the portrait of a fool. Though Little Crow was Dakota and Grandma is Ojibwa, the chasing dog is a wisdom image both tribes retain, one bridging spans of time and tribal difference.

Lake Winnibigoshish is also within the Leech Lake Ojibwa Indian Reservation. Thirteen miles across, "Winnie" is by far the largest and most dangerous lake on the Mississippi. The day I crossed it rain had reduced visibility to less than a mile and four foot swells lost their peaks to a stiff wind. Fishing season had just opened. In the shallows of the near shore, leeward of the wind, bait traps were staked to catch minnows. Willow saplings and taut netting funneled and enclosed schools of bait fish. But the traps also mark claims. Only the Ojibwa are allowed to trap on the lake. Set like spider webs in quiet places, the nets catch more than minnows. Within them lines of generations and culture are brought silently together. The traps say, "this is our home."

I'd been slowly working my way around the shoreline waiting for clearer weather. I was afraid to cross the big lake in violent weather. Several times I sheltered with the canoe under dock canopies, out of the rain. More often I alternated between paddling and baling water. There just wasn't daylight enough to paddle the shoreline round the whole lake and yet I felt compelled to reach its other side before making camp. During a lull in the storm I took note of the wind and struck for the far shore.

Minnesota is a place of hardy souls. At mid-lake I met two natives fishing. Four poles radiated from their boat as though orienting cardinal points of a compass. Though the rain had abated, the shoreline was still shrouded, invisible. I was at least unsure of my whereabouts, if not lost. The only directions I no longer questioned were up and down. Confirming my cross-lake heading, the men resumed fishing without further elaboration. When I asked if the fish were biting, I received no reply.

Five hours of beleaguered paddling situated me off Tamarack Point, my crossing's goal. By then Winnibigoshish had submitted to the evening's sulphurous clouds. The southwest wind was gaining strength again, whipping the lake into a dull reflection of the cloud's portentous grey. My canoe ran headlong, unreined amidst white-capped breakers. It galloped wildly through their peaks and troughs. Had I rested, the wind and waves would have quartered the canoe around and overturned me. Winnibigoshish was a crossing of sustained fear. I had paddled so hard for so long that my hands twitched with exhaustion. The life vest I wore was chaffing my underarms raw. They burned like flames. My shoulders, a heavy, knotted burden, ceased knowing any stroke. As I gained the point, darkness threatened with the campground still miles away. Then, to my right in the shallows, I saw more bait traps. Willow wands lifted flimsy nets thin as shadows just above the waterline. The enclosures looked like miniature water fortresses being assaulted by waves. Arrows of rain fell incessantly within their unbuttressed walls, yet they never filled.

Suddenly I knew that these enclosures, and those I'd seen on the lee shore, were throngs of magic. They were fairy rings, circles of the water spirits. They taught me not to fear the expansiveness of water or the largeness of the river. Their builders had navigated this lake and this river for thousands of years in canoes more frail than my own. Looking to the distance, at lake's end, the hulking wall of Winnibigoshish Dam blackened with each wave it swallowed. A partner to the darkness, it seemed placed there to close me in a trap of night. A counterpoint of light winked on beside the dam and then a row of yellow markers all along its face. My fear gave way to great thirst and I drank deeply from the lake.

Throughout that night storms rolled east across the lake like hellbound trains, crashing into the shoreline and my frail tent. By morning my camp was several inches deep in rainwater. Later I watched a native who worked for the Corps of Engineers open the dam's floodgates, draining Winnibigoshish of the nighttime rain. I talked to him as he worked, taking a break from portaging my gear. An eagle feather dangled from the rearview mirror of his car parked in the lot behind us. It intrigued me. I asked if it wasn't illegal to keep eagle feathers. Slapping a mosquito, he replied that the law is not normally enforced amongst natives. Leaving him I walked back toward my portaged canoe. It was gone. I was heartsick, sure that it had been stolen. Hours later I found the canoe downstream, caught in a snag.

For a brief period of time some of Minnesota's military outposts like Fort Ripley near Hole-in-the-Day's village and Fort Ridgely near Little Crow's were abandoned. The military tried to sell Fort Ripley at one point, but the highest bid was $.25 per acre, well below the minimum acceptable price of $1.25. Then, in 1857, Dakota Chief Inkapaduta massacred settlers in southern Minnesota and northern Iowa. The absence of military presence allowed Inkapaduta to escape unpunished to the western plains. His actions spurred the military to restaff both forts immediately.

Certain traders further worsened the frontier climate. They were able to manufacture claims on tribal income and expropriate huge sums because natives had no legal standing. Natives were not considered citizens in Minnesota until 1861. That year a law passed allowing natives who built cabins, tilled acreage, wore civilized dress and got haircuts to be considered for citizenship, provided they wait an additional two years. The story of William Aitkin, an early trader on the Mississippi for whom Aitkin, Minnesota is named, illustrates one effect of this denied legal standing. Aitkin, a white man, married an Ojibwa woman named Striped Cloud. Their son Alfred was murdered when he tried to reconcile a love spat between two braves, a husband and the wife's suitor. Alfred was killed by the jealous suitor. The murderer was apprehended and arraigned for trial at Prairie du Chien, the first criminal case brought under Wisconsin territorial law.

Although it was proved that Aitkin had raised his half breed son with the same care and concern that he would have devoted to a full blooded white boy, a prime factor at that time in many judicial cases where Indians were involved, the court decided it had no jurisdiction and the prisoner was acquitted."[4]

On June 4th I reached Brainerd, Minnesota spending the best part of the day in the library learning about the Hole-in-the-Days, Crow Wing and their relationship to Camp Ripley. I learned of a lost little girl and hangings, but most striking of all was the town's death toll during World War II. A large group of Brainerd's young men had enlisted as a unit in the National Guard. Forty-three of them were killed on Bataan. The town had lost only two men in the previous war. A carillon in the courthouse commemorates the lost Guardsmen each hour of the day.

Below Brainerd's Potlatch dam, and new railroad bridge, a small island divides the waters of the Mississippi. It hosts a rookery of great blue herons. These large wading birds are common the length of the river. As I left town Brainerd's herons were tending spring nests big as platforms thick in the trees. Their coarse squawks, rude landings and pinched profiles recalled primitive avians' link to reptilian ancestry. Steep river banks and the season's new foliage blocked out all of the city except the dam's high concrete walls. I portaged my canoe and re-launched it, humbled by the river, absorbed in its dam-spun currents. Beneath the walls dam gates exhausted water in foams and boils, a broth tannin-dark and vaporish-rich. Overhead, herons wheeled like a gaggle of pterodactyls survived, as though spawned from the river's fecundity. The scene was starkly primordial. The birds seemed trapped behind the dam's concrete walls, stayed from reaching the future. Brainerd's carillon chimed the sixth hour. Each note rang in perfect hollow emptiness, names repeated in litany, footfalls echoed from Bataan. They faded west like an evensong. As I paddled downstream, serenity returned to the river. Away from the dam its waters quieted. Looking behind I saw growing circles either side of my canoe's wake, no longer swirls of the dam's currents, but my own paddle prints. The river had cantored its vespers theme, I was chanting my response.

Only a couple hours of daylight remained and my map said Crow Wing State Park was twelve miles distant. The park was listed as the next and closest campsite. For me, twelve miles of river corresponds to three hours of steady paddling. I was hoping to be off the river by nightfall, away from its moving darkness and danger. A very strong wind blew in gusts from the northeast. Though the wind favored my direction, I had loaded my canoe too heavily in the forward compartment. Sharp gusts kept offsetting the stern from a straight heading, making progress slow. I began to hear strange noises passing overhead, unlike any in my experience. Each sounded with eerie, imposing suddenness at indefinite intervals. I thought it was the wind.

Once, while deer hunting years ago during a blizzard, violent whirls of wind and snow had rushed around me repeatedly. The whirls seemed like kinetic bursts triggered to my walking. They were strong enough to force down underbrush, like snow devils in random ambush. Those winter phenomena were for me yet this summer, unresolved. Approaching Crow Wing the noises I heard overhead projected the same mysterious, instant quality as the blizzard whirls. Their timing was as random. They had the same circular penetration, a compact serpentine, like the passage of a dragon, or a phoenix. Tall pines above the river's tunnel were being thrashed by the northeast wind. It swayed them in unison like a tragic chorus. The trees seemed to accompany the noises overhead, to recognize them. Listening yet more intently, I still did not understand.

Halfway to Crow Wing I was relieved to see signed above the right bank a canoe campsite marker. These signs, with their double-ended yellow-painted canoes, look like last grins of a Cheshire cat, or bananas. This one marked a site unmapped. It appeared from nowhere as though the product of my need. Here was a brand new campsite, found before darkness, a clear and level welcome. The low sun was slipping behind a high flood-bank, well back from the river. On its perfect horizon a silhouetted doe trotted through the underbrush without flagging its tail. In middle ground the campsite centered a broad terrace wide as the channel. Wind played over the sheltered glen, betrayed by waves of bending grass. A mature oak shaded the closest corner and offered half a web of roots over the water. I selected a root and tied off the canoe.

My turquoise tent seemed to almost set itself, ringed by dry, sun-bleached, prairie grasses. Nearby, a cairn of wood companioned an iron fire pit. In no time they were cooking my supper. I began to explore. Old, enameled-iron, pot-shelving unfastened from a cookstove had been planted beneath the harbor oak as a seat. Tobacco ash and leavings lay at one edge still molded to a pipe bowl's roundness. For a content moment I watched the river bend downstream through a set of rapids. Brilliant ripples coursed the river's field, catching at the evening sun. The pine gallery of the far bank swooned and overhead I heard the wind shudder again.

The cookstove shelving had been salvaged from a junk-pile, attendant spoilage to decayed and collapsing ruins of a frontier cabin. Rotted log walls tended towards the cabin's center, a broken spine of old roof. The junk-pile, once a root cellar, held other parts of the broken stove: lids and handles, legs and doors. Rusted buckets, wire and broken pottery lay beside unsalvaged remains of the stove, undisturbed in the heap. None were more than a bit of color, becoming overgrown, bowered, under reclamation by the woods. The cabin, small as a hermit's lodge, seemed long abandoned. Only its foundation was still formed in the hard lines of a man's labor.

The strange sounds in the wind continued until nightfall. As I drifted in my sleeping bag, warm over the grass, an owl hooted through the pines on the far bank, "Hooo-hoo-hoo-hoo-hoooo." Wind swept away the echoes swift as a jealous lover. But beneath it now I heard the river, constant, raised from its hard bed of stones. Not so much a groaning, more of a mumbled, trickling hymn entering the empty darkness. The river, laboring the wind, lowered the oval, smooth, owl notes into the dampened register of night's minor key. It repeated them there with assurance, like a lullaby, expectant of a new morning. I slept. In my dreams the river's voice became chimes of a carillon, then a chant, and then the image of Chief Hole-in-the-Day.

With first light I paddled toward Crow Wing. The noises overhead began again. I beached the canoe at the State Park to look around and get drinking water. The wind was gone and in morning's new air the soundings were close and clear. A park worker drove a tractor out of the woods mowing a swath into the clearing at the river's edge. He was wrapped in khaki green from head to toe against a cloud of mosquitoes that followed him like a plague. I asked him about the noises. Leaning down from his seat, above the tractor's engine roar and the whining mower blade, from behind his face netting and dark sunglasses, he told me the noises were artillery rounds. Across the river at Camp Ripley, gunners were raining on the practice range.

The MDNR Trails and Waterways office maintains canoe access campsites along the Mississippi headwaters. They publish a useful set of river maps that detail campsite locations and distances, portages, drinking water, rapids and dams. Notes for the section around Camp Ripley included mention of Crow Wing, Hole-in-the-Day's village, describing it as one of Minnesota's oldest ghost towns. Crow Wing was abandoned in 1871 when the Northern Pacific Railroad bridged the river ten miles upstream at Brainerd. The railroad and Crow Wing's leading landholder, Clement Beaulieu, couldn't price a crossing, so the railroad went north. With it went all the people, and the future, of Crow Wing. Crow Wing State Park commemorates the trading post run by Beaulieu and Walker. Beaulieu's mansion was the site of an archaeology dig the summer of my journey. Interns from Mankato State were sifting soils there when I visited. The students wore shorts and went sleeveless, somehow untroubled by the plague of mosquitoes. They had staked out the foundation of Beaulieu's mansion and were commencing a layered trench "dig" with trowels and shovels. I was shown a small bag of artifacts they'd uncovered. There were bits of glass and broken cup, rusted nails and a piece of comb.

Fort Ripley of the frontier has evolved into a modern-day National Guard Camp. From my canoe, along the camp's river perimeter I read signs, "No Trespassing—Property of the U.S. Government." Tracks of amphibious vehicles had torn cleated prints into the river bank. Steel cables elevated on either side by heavy pylons sagged to barely a man's height above the water, apparatus for aerial crossings. There was a gravel lot parked around with camouflaged and armored vehicles. Standing and loitering in a throb of dust I saw a clot of uniformed men. The dust rose everywhere around them, departing westward in a plume that marked the road. Adjacent to the lot a concrete embankment aproned into the water. Moorings big enough to hawse a ship bordered its vertical edges. But mostly the camp appeared as simple wilderness from another time. I saw more deer, raccoon, geese, and other wildlife on Camp Ripley than anywhere else the length of the river.

The law bound, bent and punished natives in protection of whites, but it offered them no refuge from murderers, much less thieving traders. By August 1862 the situation at Minnesota's Indian agencies was ripe for explosion. When Dakota annuity payments failed to arrive by late summer traders Andrew and Nathan Myrick cut off credit. The Myrick brothers were partners in an extended string of trading posts throughout the north, including my hometown, La Crosse, Wisconsin. Nathan is revered as our city's founder. The brothers were successful in raking fat shares of 1851 and 1858 treaty settlements, as well as subsequent annuity payments. Andrew Myrick operated the Lower Agency post near New Ulm on the Minnesota River which served the Dakotas. James Lynd, the debauchee and occasional spiritual observer of Dakotas, was his assistant. The Myricks knew the Dakotas were desperate to the point of starvation. They leveraged that desperate condition into political pressure on the government, hoping to force quicker release of annuity funds. When the brothers cut off credit they enjoined other traders to do the same. They argued that stern action was needed to break the bureaucratic holdup. A Dakota interpreter petitioned Andrew Myrick for food on behalf of the tribe. In the presence of several braves Myrick replied, "Let them eat grass," adding in the spirit of the frontier, "or their own dung." The interpreter hesitated, but ultimately translated Myrick's remark to the Dakota. The effect was incendiary. Like James Lynd, Andrew Myrick became an early victim of the U.S.-Dakota Conflict. Killed in the first battle, his body was found weeks later by his brother Nathan. It bore several arrows and the blade of a hay scythe. He had been shot repeatedly and scalped. From his own mouth came the Dakota's answer to Andrew's parsimonious insult: it had been stuffed with a bunch of dried grass.

Both the Ojibwa and Dakotas had been cheated and starved. Their ties to agents, traders and settlers were tensioned to extreme limits by immoral, corrupt and ignorant behavior. Annuity payments due to arrive had been postponed in Washington and political maneuverings at St. Paul further delayed distribution. Patronage appointments following Lincoln's election kept agency relations in turmoil. The Civil War drained away professional soldiers, weakening U.S. military presence at Forts Ripley and Ridgely. Traders colluding with politicians bilked the tribes and cut off their credit. Separated by miles of wilderness and ages of warfare, both tribes were primed to detonate. The events which triggered their respective revolts were different, though similar. For the Dakota it was a general insult to the whole tribe. For the Ojibwa, the affront was personal.

President Lincoln's personal secretary, John G. Nicolay, was visiting Minnesota at the time of the Conflict. Here is his account of the personal event that incensed Chief Hole-in-the-Day:

> A quarrel had gradually grown up between him (Hole-in-the-Day) and the Indian agent of the Chippewas. Hole-in-the-Day determined to get rid of the Agent, went to Washington, and preferred charges of fraud and corruption against him. An investigation was promised, and he returned home. Pending the delay two of his braves went to the Agency and killed several cattle. This incensed the Agent, who, in turn, sent an order to the military commandant of Fort Ripley to have the chief arrested. A file of soldiers was started to execute the order...Hole-in-the-Day, however, saw the proceeding from an eminence, hurried home to his house, quickly put his squaws and children into several canoes, and started across the Mississippi River just as the soldiers came up. They leveled their guns at the party, and ordered Hole-in-the-Day to stop and surrender himself. He did not obey; but pushing across the river, leaped out of his canoe, drew his pistol, and fired

at the soldiers, who promptly returned the shots...Enraged at the attempt to arrest him, and at being fired upon, he at once dispatched runners to the different bands of the Chippewas at Leech Lake, at Otter Tail Lake, and at Rabbit Lake, to kill all the whites, rob their stores and dwellings and join him at once with their warriors at Gull Lake...[5]

The Ojibwa destroyed property and took prisoners but they didn't kill anyone. Lucius C. Walker, Indian agent at Crow Wing, the trading post nearest Gull Lake, panicked when Hole-in-the-Day's arrest failed. Fleeing to St. Cloud he chanced to meet Commissioner of Indian Affairs William P. Dole, and John G. Nicolay, Lincoln's secretary. Dole and Nicolay, both from Washington, were together in St. Cloud by happenstance. Dole had come west to negotiate a treaty with Ojibwa bands north of Gull Lake; Nicolay was on holiday. At their meeting Walker became incoherent in his account of Hole-in-the-Day's actions. Victimized by his own fear, he left St. Cloud completely deranged, bound for Fort Snelling downstream at Minneapolis. The agent carried in his cargo four kegs of gold and silver, payroll originally intended for troops at Fort Ripley. Accompanied by armed guards, he spread general pandemonium among Mississippi valley settlers with news that Hole-in-the-Day had joined Little Crow's revolt, begun only days earlier. Neither he nor the payroll ever reached Fort Snelling. He was found dead and alone, a presumed suicide. Unsurprisingly, the payroll had disappeared.

Commissioner Dole, by virtue of his office, reluctantly took command of the U.S. role in the Ojibwa Conflict. He engaged George W. Sweet and Clement H. Beaulieu, Sr. to parley with Hole-in-the-Day at Gull Lake. Sweet and Beaulieu were well known to the Ojibwa. Beaulieu was the former trader at Crow Wing. He had lost his license to trade after Lincoln's election, replaced by Walker. Looking back on that day at Crow Wing now I have to smile. When I was turning those little broken pieces of history from Beaulieu's mansion over in my palm I had no sense of his politics. It seems curious that a man unfit to trade was so easily qualified to parley.

Sweet, Beaulieu, and Father Francis Xavier Pierz, a Catholic missionary, went to Gull Lake to petition Hole-in-the-Day for peace. They were refused admittance because the chief had circled the village with an imaginary line saying, "Let no man cross this line and live." Undaunted, Father Pierz persisted until braves carried him over the line, thus superseding Hole-in-the-Day's order. All three emissaries had strong bonds of trust among the Gull Lake band. Eventually they were successful in convincing Hole-in-the-Day to make truce. He released captive settlers and agreed to meet with Commissioner Dole. There followed a series of appointments and cancellations. Both sides had reason to delay negotiations. Hole-in-the-Day awaited the outcome of events under Little Crow, while Dole, because of the Civil War, had trouble commandeering troops to accompany him.

Finally, on September 15, Hole-in-the-Day and Dole faced one another at Crow Wing. Hole-in-the-Day knew the Dakota were faring poorly against the U.S. For his part, Dole had secured troops, but they were few and inexperienced. At the initial meeting Hole-in-the-Day outmaneuvered Dole, badly embarrassing him. By military feint the chief's warriors surrounded Dole's forces in overwhelming numbers. The warriors openly flourished their weapons and throughout the council made menacing gestures. Later Commissioner Dole would report that Hole-in-the-Day was trying to blackmail him during the negotiations. I suspect that's true. Among Hole-in-the-Day's demands was a $10,000 personal payment. But I wonder if blackmail wasn't a secondary objective. I think Hole-in-the-Day's primary objective was survival for his tribe. To accomplish that he threatened Dole's life. Surrounded by warriors, Dole must have felt very empty before Hole-in-the-Day. For that little while the Commissioner was forced to truly listen. In that moment, though the bargain was unspoken, Hole-in-the-Day exchanged Dole's life for survival of his tribe. There followed his outrageous demands for blackmail. After a few days the other chiefs and warriors grew tired and jealous of Hole-in-the-Day's machinations. Some began separate negotiations and eventually everyone just went home.

There is a bluff one and a half miles northeast of Little Falls, Minnesota named after Hole-in-the-Day. The elder chief is said to be buried there. Younger Hole-in-the-Day slept on the grave one night, dreamed, and afterwards predicted his own death. Today, no one knows where younger Hole-in-the-Day rests. He was supposedly buried in the Catholic cemetery at Crow Wing, but efforts to disinter him found no remains. Ironically, that area near Little Falls and Crow Wing, burial site of the great Ojibwa dynasty, was once the center of the Dakota tribe.

The nominal leader of the Dakota during the Conflict was Little Crow, known to his own people as Ta-o-ya-te-du-ta, "His Scarlet People." He was a chief of the Mdewankanton band, the last of at least four others of the same name in a dynasty centuries old. His ancient chain antedated any historical recording begun with European arrival. The Little Crow dynasty, originally at Kaposia and south of Minneapolis, was moved west to New Ulm on the Minnesota river by the Treaty of 1851. There Little Crow was chief and remained so until after the Treaty of 1858. His people considered that treaty a failure and held Little Crow accountable. Discontent cost Little Crow his chieftanship. In his place, Wabasha, who had refused to negotiate or sign the treaty, was elected head chief. When the Conflict began however, Chief Wabasha wanted no part of the violence ignited by Shakopee's braves. Shakopee and others of the Soldier's Lodge turned to Little Crow. Knowing Little Crow still coveted his old authority they drafted him as war chief. The Conflict would later become known as a massacre, but Little Crow did not prosecute it as such. Shakopee and other radicals committed the worst native atrocities. At the height of hostilities Little Crow sheltered captive settlers in his own home.

Consider Little Crow's words spoken in the Soldier's Lodge council, one of his people's democratic bodies, on the eve of the Dakota Conflict. On hand were young braves who had already killed a family of settlers. They wanted Little Crow to condone their actions with his authority. Taunting him as a coward they shamed him into accepting a role as war chief. First he blackened his face in mourning. Then he said,

> Ta-o-ya-te-du-ta is not a coward, and he is not a fool! When did he run away from his enemies? When did he leave his braves behind him on a war-path and turn back to his tepees? When he ran away from your enemies, he walked behind on your trail with his face to the Ojibways and covered your backs as a she-bear covers her cubs! Is Ta-o-ya-te-du-ta without scalps? Look at his war feathers! Behold the scalp-locks of your enemies hanging there on his lodge-poles! Do they call him a coward? Ta-o-ya-te-du-ta is not a coward, and he is not a fool. Braves, you are like little children; you know not what you are doing.
>
> You are full of white man's devil-water (rum). You are like dogs in the Hot Moon when they run mad and snap at their own shadows. We are only little herds of buffaloes left scattered; the great herds that once covered the prairies are no more. See!-the white men are like locusts when they fly so thick that the whole sky is a snowstorm. You may kill one-two-ten; yes, as many as the leaves in the forest yonder, and their brothers will not miss them. Kill one-two-ten, and ten times ten will come to kill you. Count on your fingers all day

long and white men with guns in their hands will come faster than you can count. Yes; they fight among themselves- away off. Do you hear the thunder of their big guns? No; it would take you two moons to run down to where they are fighting, and all the way your path would be among the white soldiers as thick as tamaracks in the swamps of the Ojibways. Yes; they fight among themselves, but if you strike at them they will all turn on you and devour you and your women and little children just as the locusts in their time fall on the trees and devour all the leaves in one day. You cannot see the face of your chief; your eyes are full of smoke. You cannot hear his voice; your ears are full of roaring waters. Braves, you are little children—you are fools. You will die like rabbits when the hungry wolves hunt them in the Hard Moon (January). Ta-o-ya-te-du-ta is not a coward: he will die with you.[6]

Little Crow led the young braves into the U.S.-Dakota Conflict and it ended as he predicted. General Sibley and his troops hunted the Dakota out of Minnesota. Many Dakota died. Little Crow's Mdewankanton band, the "people of the lakes," were forcibly deported in 1863. But the Mississippi still clutches momentos of its first people, especially those last taken. Seven villages of Mdewankanton were once clustered on the Mississippi, all in Minnesota: Kiyuksa near present-day Winona, Khemnichan the present-day Red Wing, Kaposia meaning "light-footed" near South St. Paul and Canoska, Hayataotonwan, Oyataysheeka and Tintonwan. These last four were located on the Minnesota river, from Shakopee downstream to the Mississippi, today's metropolitan Minneapolis.

Another Mdewankanton Dakota dynasty was the Shakopee, "Little Six" in English. The city of Shakopee, Minnesota just west of Minneapolis is named for them. The last of their dynasty, Eat-o-ka, "Another Language," took the name Shakopee at his father's death. By some he was considered a moron. In any case he and his band were among the most vicious natives during the U.S.-Dakota Conflict. Four of his band killed settlers at Acton, Minnesota, igniting the hostilities. Shakopee fled to Canada after the Conflict. He was kidnapped there in 1864, returned to Minneapolis, and hung.

The Red Wing (Koo-poo-hoo-sha) dynasty was also among the oldest on the river. Extending back before the Revolution, at least four generations of these Mdewankanton Dakota chiefs lived in the village at the top of Lake Pepin. Their village has become the present city of Red

Wing. Legend has Wakuta Red Wing buried bestride his horse in the bluff above the city. His son Wacouta, the "Leaf Shooter," succeeded him to become a reluctant participant in the Dakota Conflict. Red Wing was closely allied with chief Wabasha. Like Wabasha he and his band were moved to Nebraska following the Conflict. He died shortly afterwards.

There were Winnebago and Ojibwa villages as well. While the names of their native villages are all but forgotten, their leaders names are still familiar. Most of the dynasties were broken during the Minnesota Conflict, channeled by a bit of history that was hard, sharp and short. The dynastic names and spirits of the native leaders were driven into the earth and enclosed there, extinct, and therefore permanent. As though to give perfect witness, the Mississippi took those names as its own and imprinted them along its length. Winneshiek, Decorah, Waukon, Red Wing, Wabasha, Shakopee, and the scene of the final act, Mankato, are only some of the names. Through these names and the events tied to the Conflict, one begins to learn the river. Learning the river reveals its spirit. Acknowledging that spirit America looks back upon itself, within itself, to know itself, to know its own name.

The river's order engenders wonder. Much is seen, but much more can only be sensed. Much is below the surface, moving, moved, fixed in place yet still in motion. Memory, experience and prescience are both the river's burden and its essence. It pours empty places full as surely as day fills empty night. It has a single need, that some place first be made empty. There in that empty place the river swirls, deposits and erodes, fulfilling itself, remaking itself. It makes new emptiness, immense, continuous, and wonderful. The river collects events from history with profound disrespect for time and place. It deposits what it will, and where. These deposits are ordered neither chronologically nor geographically. Consider that deep in Louisiana several channel navigation markers at the Old River Control Structure are named for Black Hawk. Black Hawk is the predominant native personality of the upper Mississippi and the subject of the next chapter, "The Adventures of Injun' Joe." His era predated the Minnesota conflicts and his influence colored those events. No evidence suggests he was ever so far south as Louisiana. Yet Louisiana is where the river continues to hold his name, over a thousand miles south of his home. The river has carried him there to be its own vigilant, ironic and perhaps vengeful sentinel. For years now Black Hawk has watched the Army Corps of Engineers spend billions of dollars warring the river, as it once warred with him.

Black Hawk was practically related to the Winneshieks through his shaman, the Winnebago Prophet. The Mississippi's Lake Winneshiek, south of Lansing, Iowa is named for these dynastic chiefs. Like Black Hawk, an elder Winneshiek fought with the British in the War of 1812. Later Wakan-ja-ko-ga, his son, joined Black Hawk with sons of his own in Black Hawk's War. Afterwards, young Winneshiek and his two sons were imprisoned alongside Black Hawk and the Prophet at Jefferson Barracks, Missouri. That Winneshiek was made chief by government appointment in 1845. His band was forced to move from Wisconsin to Long Prairie, Minnesota in 1850, and then in 1855 to Blue Earth, Minnesota, very near the area of the U.S.-Dakota Conflict. In 1859 Winneshiek was removed as chief for insubordination. The government wanted chiefs who were non-chiefs. Winneshiek's testimony is revealing even today.

> White men have gone to our land and cut some of our best timber-which was valuable to us, and our agent did not prevent the trespassers, and when I spoke to him about it, he said, "never mind, they won't cut anymore," so I can't but believe that the agent sold the timber.[7]

Winneshiek's oldest son, Hounk-ka, "The Chief," along with about a dozen other Winnebagoes participated in the Dakota Conflict. For this token participation, the band suffered brutal removal to Fort Thompson, South Dakota in May, 1863. Winneshiek and several hundred followers abandoned that reservation within months to move yet again, this time to Nebraska. In 1872 he died attempting to return to his original home in Wisconsin. A son who took his name, Little Winneshiek, did return. He died in 1920 at Black River Falls, Wisconsin.

Waukon Decorah and his brother, One Eyed Decorah, also Winnebagoes, fought against Blackhawk in 1832. One Eyed Decorah accompanied Black Hawk to his surrender. Their Decorah name adorns cities, counties, bluffs and streams throughout the area adjoined by Iowa, Minnesota, and Wisconsin on the Mississippi. They were related to Winneshiek through a common French ancestor, Sobrevoie DeCarrie. Waukon's son, Maw-he-coo-sha-na-zhe-kaw, became the most famous of the dynasty. His name means "he who stands with his head reaching the clouds," but he was known as Little Decorah. Little Decorah counseled strongly against Winnebago involvement in the U.S.-Dakota Conflict. Though his band remained peaceful, they too were moved afterwards, first to Fort Thompson, South Dakota, then to Nebraska. He died near Portage, Wisconsin in 1887 survived by a son, Tall Decorah, who died a year later.

One of the oldest Dakota dynasties on the upper river was Wabasha. The name is derived from Dakota words "wape" for leaf, and "sha" for red. It refers to the red color of burr-oak leaves in fall. The present-day city of Wabasha is located just south of the confluence of the Chippewa and Mississippi rivers at the foot of Lake Pepin. The Wabasha's original village was near contemporary Winona, Minnesota. They were chiefs of the Mdewankanton Dakota and fought against Black Hawk. Joseph Wabasha had been elected general chief at the time of the U.S.-Dakota Conflict. Though he argued in council for peace, the tribe was governed democratically. The Soldier's Lodge favored war and they prevailed. Wabasha retained his position as civil chief, but Little Crow was drafted to lead the warriors. Wabasha witnessed many of the battles as a noncombatant. He worked and counseled actively for peace. After the Conflict he gave this testimony:

> The Great Father (President Franklin Pierce) told me, before leaving, that he wished us to be well off, but that the whites would endeavor to get this land from us, and that traders were like rats; they would use all their endeavors to steal our substance, and that if we were wise we would never sign a paper for anyone. If we did so we would never see ten cents for all our property. I remembered the words of our Great Father and I knew that they were true. I was consequently always afraid of traders.
>
> Two years after this, when we had gathered our corn, we all went out on the fall hunt for furs. After we had been out some time the traders, the most active of whom was Mr. [Nathan?] Myrick, sent out for the chief to come in to sign papers for him in reference to selling the land on the north side of the Minnesota River [1858]. I refused to go in. The others, I am told, went home and signed some papers and received for doing so, horses, guns, blankets, and other articles. They told me this after I came home. I always refused to sign papers for the traders, and therefore they hated me. By the result of this paper signed without my consent or knowledge, the traders obtained possession of all the money coming from the sale of the land on the north side of the Minnesota River, and also half of our annuity for the year 1862.[8]

After the Conflict, Wabasha's band was moved to Santee Agency, Nebraska where he died in 1876.

Wabasha's complaint against traders was not spurious. In 1851 a major land cession treaty sold Dakota territory in southern Minnesota to the U.S. Government. One treaty provision specified cash payments of $385,000 to Dakotas in "open council." Instead, Governor Ramsey and his appointed administrator, Hugh Tyler, distributed $320,000 to themselves, friends and traders behind closed doors. This theft raised such protest that in 1857 the Indian Department in Washington appointed Major Kitzing Pritchette to investigate. He substantiated the fraud wrought by Ramsey, Tyler and the traders, but it did no good. The following year Dakotas were enticed to sell additional lands, attracting more fraud. When treaty funds were finally distributed, the Dakotas received nothing. In fact, traders had fabricated and inflated claims to such extent that the Dakotas actually owed money. This was the infamous Treaty of 1858, the one Wabasha refused to sign.

Native loyalties during the U.S.-Dakota Conflict were divided. Before the crisis, bands, villages and individuals were falling away from traditional practices that had sustained communal harmony. Growing dependence upon the government, traders and settlers marked the period. When the crisis came, dynastic leaders were forced into dilemma. Winneshiek, Decorah, Wabasha and Red Wing chose the path of assimilation, submission and peace: Shakopee, Sleepy Eye and Little Crow walked the traditional path of resistance, bloodshed and war. Little Crow's words, "Ta-o-ya-te-du-ta is not a coward: he will die with you," probably expressed the thoughts of many who chose the path of war. Though he was not a coward, neither was he courageous. Courage does not take the path of fools.

Little Crow's path seems one of inconsistencies. He was war chief, but he responded readily to General Sibley's overtures for peace. He sought rapprochement more vigorously than victory. He led charges against Fort Ridgely yet protected captives in his own home. He counseled against war yet intended to die fighting. There was an unmistakable duality in the words and actions of Little Crow, and yet perhaps elements of balance as well. Perhaps he found himself at the fulcrum of two cultures and was unable to choose between them. By upbringing and lineage he was prejudiced toward war. By nature and experience he was drawn toward peace. He tried to accommodate both disciplines, however poorly. As he acknowledged, the moment of power was decidedly against his people. Yet he weighed his own authority onto the platen of hostility. He accepted the most brutal of all measures, a contest of war. The resulting violence proved his prophetic words of doom too limited. Consequences of the Conflict consumed many more than his own band. The peaceful dynasties of Wabasha, Red Wing, Decorah and Winneshiek were drawn into the same furnace. Their people were counted in company with Little Crow. In the madness following the U.S.-Dakota Conflict, all of Minnesota's Dakota and Winnebago were moved away and ended.

Today some of the Mdewankanton have returned. Four hundred thirty tribal members live on Prairie Island, a small reservation on the Mississippi near Red Wing, Minnesota. They still struggle. Northern States Power, a regional utility company, is their modern nemesis. The company seeks to store spent nuclear fuel in casks at a site adjacent to the reservation. But the tribe doesn't want the waste nearby. They passed an ordinance prohibiting transport of nuclear waste on reservation roads, the only access to the storage site. Recently the company purchased neighboring property to construct a new road. Joe Campbell, a tribal member, speaks, writes letters and encourages people to join his group, the Downstream Alliance. The Alliance hopes to stop Northern States Power. For decades the river has cooled power plants and nuclear reactors. Perhaps the river is also ready to accept spent fuel with a half-life of eons. Joe Campbell and the Mdewankanton are not.

Knowledge of the Minnesota Conflicts spread like a prairie wildfire. Settlers throughout the upper Midwest became alarmed. Panic spread east as far as Milwaukee and south well into Iowa. Frightened settlers barricaded or abandoned homes, some never returned. In little over a month the U.S.-Dakota conflict claimed the lives of nearly five hundred settlers. For the Dakota, deaths went mostly unrecorded, except for those hung. At the Conflicts' end a military tribunal convicted and condemned over three hundred Dakotas. But final say rested with President Abraham Lincoln. Very few people entreated Lincoln to show mercy, though Anglican Bishop Whipple was one. Whipple was a contemporary of Reverend Gilfillan. He wrote the president an open letter and published "AN APPEAL FOR THE RED MAN."

> I am sick at heart; I fear the words of one of our statesmen to be true; "Bishop, every word you say of this Indian system is true: the nation knows it. It is useless, you will not be heard. Your faith is only like that of the man that stood on the bank of the river waiting for the water to run by that he might cross over dry shod." All I have to say is, that if a nation trembling on the brink of anarchy and ruin is so dead that it will not hear a plea to redress wrongs which the whole people admit call for reform, God in mercy pity us and our children.[9]

But the tenor of the day was better captured by John G. Nicolay, Lincoln's personal secretary:

> In their present location, the feud of race engendered by the insurrection will only die with the generation that witnessed its beginning. Humanitarian impulses and humanitarian duties are forgotten in the fierce thirst for private vengeance. With one voice, the people of that State demand removal or threaten the extermination of their dangerous neighbors.[10]

In the end Lincoln wrote an order to the military commission that they "...cause to be executed the following named, to wit...". There followed a list of thirty-nine people. Lincoln himself wrote out each Indian name. At the very end he wrote his own. Later, one of the thirty-nine received clemency. The others were hung en masse at Mankato, Minnesota the day after Christmas, 1863. It has been called "America's Greatest Mass Execution"; a boy survivor of the Conflict tripped the scaffold.

Little Crow was not among those hung. He evaded capture by going west with several hundred followers. His band gradually dispersed until only his son accompanied him. The two were trying to steal horses near Hutchinson, Minnesota on July 3, 1863 when confronted by settlers. Though his son escaped unharmed, Little Crow was killed. He was scalped and his body was thrown into a pit of slaughter offal.

> About a week afterward the head was pushed off with a stick, and left lying on the prairie for several days, the brains oozing out in the broiling sun. It was afterward picked up and deposited in a kettle of lime preparatory to a process to render it suitable for a place in the rooms of the Historical Society, and the body was thrown into the river, to remain until the flesh sloughed off, and the bones were in a condition for preservation.[11]

Chief Hole-in-the Day fared a little better. He lived until June 27, 1868. Braves of the Pillager Band, his own people, assassinated him from behind on his way home from Crow Wing. Jealousy was thought to be their motive. In 1864 Hole-in-the-Day had traveled to Washington and received $5,000 for a new house and $1,000 in yearly stipend from Commissioner Dole. Perhaps the braves were jealous of

Hole-in-the-Day's "blackmail" payments. But four years seems a long time for jealousy to fester into action. There is another theory. At the time of his murder Hole-in-the-Day was planning another trip to Washington. He wanted to protest Ojibwa treatment at the hand of their new government agent. The agent, prompted by lumber interests, was trying to force resettlement of Hole-in-the-Day's band. When he learned that Hole-in-the-Day would be petitioning Washington for his removal, the agent hired Pillagers as assassins. That conspiracy theory was not investigated; the murders of natives seldom were.

It seems uncanny that both Dakota and Ojibwa revolted simultaneously. Common wisdom holds no communication between them during the Conflicts, yet both undertook action virtually the same day. Surely similar beliefs, traditions and conditions focused each tribe's attention in a similar manner. But that they reacted in the same moment suggests something more to me. The something more may have been a sign, simple as a shared dream, or wonderful as the breath of the Great Mysterious.

The Plains Indian Wars began in Minnesota with the Conflict of 1862. They ended in Minnesota, too, at the century's end, with the "Last Indian War." The Ojibwa were being cheated by lumber barons, which was nothing new. On October 5, 1898, the Pillager Band fought Brevet-Major Melville C. Wilkerson at Leech Lake Indian Reservation. Wilkerson and five of his men were killed and nine others wounded. Later the Ojibwas were convicted. Then on January 3, 1899 President McKinley issued pardons. The chief who had encouraged the braves to follow their hearts, even to fight if necessary, had a name which commanded great respect. Thirty years after his nominative's death, here was yet another Chief Hole-in-the-Day.

Now, like all origin stories, the story of Hole-in-the-Day comes full circle. First, hole-in-the-day is a fissure in the dome of the sky, an entryway for light. Then, Hole-in-the-Day is a dynasty which leads the Ojibwa people. Finally, the resting place of Hole-in-the-Day glimpses into the life beyond, one amongst ancestors in a beautiful country. Presumably, there too, light streams through a fissure, a hole-in-the-day.

Along Minnesota Highway 2, just east of the headwaters, a big, blue, reflective highway sign points the Bug-O-Nay-Ge-Shig exit with official boldness. There, just outside Cass Lake, a modern complex owned by the Ojibwa tribe, including a bingo parlor and school, are named Bug-O-Nay-Ge-Shig. The sign appears like some kind of elementary phonic spelling lesson. The syllables, unfamiliar to me, are displayed as though drawn one-by-one from a mouth unwilling to speak them. The first syllable, Bug, is almost an affront. How could anything significant begin so inconsequentially? When I began my river trip, Bug-O-Nay-Ge-Shig was a meaningless, perhaps archaic word for me. I did not know it was a man's name. But in the course of endless paddlestrokes I came to know the river. One sun empty day, near the source of the Mississippi, Bug-O-Nay-Ge-Shig was born. In English his name is Hole-in-the-Day.

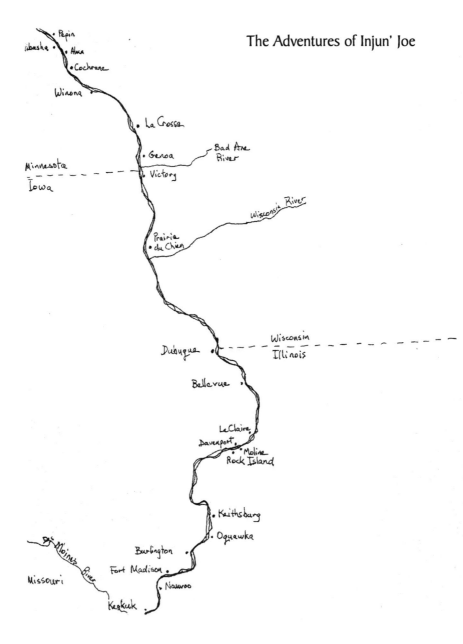

The Adventures of Injun' Joe

Pepin
Wabasha • • Alma
• Cochrane
Winona •

La Crossa •

Bad Axe
River

• Genoa

Minnesota
Iowa
• Victory

Wisconsin River

Prairie
• du Chien

Wisconsin
Dubuque • Illinois

Bellevue •

LeClaire •
Davenport •
• Moline
Rock Island

• Keithsburg

• Oquawka

Des Moines River
Burlington •
Fort Madison •
Missouri
• Nauvoo
Keokuk •

The Adventures of Injun' Joe

When I began this trip I promised myself a Bombay Sapphire Gin martini if I could make it to the Harborview Café. The Café is on the Wisconsin side of Lake Pepin, five hundred miles downstream from Lake Itasca. Its bookstore-dining room looks west over a sailboat harbor and across the lake into Minnesota's bluffs. Well, I made it. I telephoned friends in Alma and Cochrane who joined me at the Café to celebrate. It was a homecoming of sorts. The long-awaited martini was delicious and my friends spectacular. Before long I was feeling rosy as a sunset. For fun, one of my friends, an attorney, pulled a Mexican cookbook down from the shelf above our table. He selected a recipe at random and began declaiming it in his best courtroom style. The topic, oddly appropriate, was dressing an octopus for dinner. There were instructions on avoiding the beak, the egg sac and most enlightening for me, the ink. Imagine dressing an animal with eight arms and a supply of ink. What a distressing beast to meet at dinner.

Two days later I was really home, in La Crosse. I'd let my house for the summer to an immigrant couple, refugees from Southeast Asia. They hosted me like a brother while I prepared to continue my journey. Up until that point I had leap-frogged my car along, fetching it every day or so on my bicycle. It was packed with every bit of outdoor gear I owned. The car served as a mobile storehouse and refuge, my perambulator. But shuttling was a burden and most of the stuff never got used. On returning home I sorted out essential camping gear and packed it into a single waterproof duffel. I put my charts, food and other items in plastic boxes. The car had gone as far as it was going to go. I retired it to the garage.

Repacked and reprovisioned, I planned to resume my trip the morning of July first. After a fitful night I awoke with a sour stomach, sweating, shaken by a nightmare. Still half asleep I wondered if I'd become afraid of the river. People often asked me if I was frightened out there. I always replied no, that I respected the river, but wasn't afraid of it. Gradually, as I grew more awake, details of my nightmare flooded back. A white station wagon carrying a woman and her daughters had careened past me down a steep, wooded hill. The car was old, badly rusted, the fenders about to flap off. Near the bottom of the hill the car hit a tree head-on and stopped, dust rising all around it. I ran after it, stumbling, anxious to offer help. The mother staggered from her car, drawing one of the girls after her. They fell to the ground where the woman cradled her daughter's head in her lap. Both were badly hurt and bleeding. The other daughter remained in the car, sitting upright with her eyes open. For some reason I assumed she was dead. A man I recognized approached the pieta of wounded women in the same moment as I. He was smiling and very calm. To my horror he put a pistol to the girl's temple and fired. Horrible as it was, the act seemed one of mercy and then, thankfully, I awakened.

My renter had shown me a .38 Special the night before. He kept it in the house, loaded. Over breakfast coffee, on the way to the river, I told him that the gun had to go. We had problems understanding one another. I think he was trying to tell me he would keep the gun unloaded. I didn't care. I'd never dreamt such an awful or compelling dream. I told him several times that the gun had to be taken out of my house. Then, mercifully, I was back on the river.

The water's steady flow felt stable, powerful and reassuring. Flowing at constant speed in a single direction it was simplicity itself. The only needful thing from me was to observe and be still. By comparison my household had been chaotic. I wondered if I knew what home meant anymore. Being with people, remembering them, finding their real meanings: people were not like the river. Paddling away from the landing I truly left La Crosse. It felt like my journey was beginning for the first time. The river was becoming my home.

At a park south of town I stopped to re-check my gear one last time and to use the toilet. I tied off to a small tree and climbed the bank, a rip-rap mess of broken concrete. Beside the park's outer drive a man lay on the ground, sleeping. He'd rolled out of his bedding onto the grass. Dried clippings flecked his dusty hair, gingham shirt, blue jeans and socks. An old pick-up was parked nearby, picketed like a horse. It, too, was dusty, flecked with rust and well worn. The windshield was cracked and the license plates from out of state. A battered suitcase lay open on the front seat, spilling clothes onto the floorboards. Styrofoam cups, paper wrappers and fast food bags littered the cab. The ashtray was a jointed, grey mound of bent filters. On the dash were old books of matches, a spinning reel and a pair of sunglasses. I walked toward the toilets wondering if this man were the sort of vagabond that I would become. The toilets were padlocked, so I climbed back down the jumbled concrete. I relieved myself against the little tree and untethered the canoe. Rummaging in the forward compartment I found my sunglasses. I put them on and crouched to work the canoe's bow around to point downstream. Then I pushed off from the bank and stepped back into the current.

> A passing Winnebago hunter found their camp and without their knowing it hurried downstream to inform the Winnebago leaders...the chief persuaded his council that they should send messengers with a calumet to the fugitives. If they accepted and smoked the pipe, the Winnebagoes would ask the group to end the war, and under Indian custom the Sauks would have to agree.[12]

The Sauks in this case were members of Black Hawk's Band. Black Hawk, at age sixty-five, was an old warrior wandering away from bitter defeat. As a boy of thirteen, during the Revolutionary War, his village had been burned on orders from America's General of the West, George Rogers Clark. Since then Black Hawk had struck many times against the new nation. The scene above, in August 1832, describes his last moments of resistance. His band by then was all but wiped out. The Winnebagoes seeking him were neutral, but were under pressure by the government to help capture the old warrior. Later, when they returned to his camp with a calumet, Black Hawk refused its offering of peace. A boy in his party, amidst loud protests from Sauk elders, took the Winnebago pipe and smoked. His act bound all the Sauk to seek peace. Black Hawk honored the pipe's tradition and followed the Winnebago to their village at La Crosse. He rested a few days while women there prepared new garments for him to wear. Then, clad in full length white buckskins, Black Hawk traveled to Prairie du Chien, Wisconsin and surrendered.

Black Hawk's own village, Saukenuk, is now the city of Rock Island, Illinois. The surrounding complex which includes Davenport and Bettendorf, Iowa and Moline, Illinois is known today as the Quad Cities. Their precursor, Saukenuk, lay three miles above the Mississippi on the Rock River. In those days the Mississippi fell over two sets of rapids, bracketing Rock Island. The island and its nearby village, lying between the rapids, were a popular landing. Its occupants and trade were courted in turn by the French, the Spanish, the English and finally the Americans. Black Hawk's people had migrated to Saukenuk from Montréal some one hundred years before his birth. They had been driven from the Great Lakes by the westward push of colonization and wars with neighboring tribes. Ultimately Black Hawk would be pushed as well, first into war and then, in defeat, westward, across the Mississippi. There he would live out his remaining days relatively quietly. He even wrote an autobiography.

Black Hawk is the best known personality on the river, except Mark Twain. Certainly Twain is more widely read. Their stories have common links, most obviously the river. But differences are just as obvious. Black Hawk's story preceded Twain's and is not fictitious. He dictated his autobiography two years before Samuel Clemens, who later became Mark Twain, was born. Saukenuk, Black Hawk's village, was about one hundred eighty miles above Twain's hometown, Hannibal, Missouri. Devil's Creek, Iowa, where Black Hawk spent his last years and died, is less than seventy. While Twain's locale is these days overrun with literary tourists, not so Black Hawk's. He is remembered as a warrior, not a writer.

Begun in June 1832, Black Hawk's War was finished in the dog days of August. It ended in massacre at Battle Island, just downstream from Victory, Wisconsin on the Mississippi. So many Sauk were killed so quickly that the river was dyed red with their blood. Black Hawk survived, surrendered and was imprisoned. Later he was taken East and sentenced during audience with President Andrew Jackson. After brief captivity he was toured through the principal cities to impress upon him the power of those he had opposed. Returned to the Mississippi, he was placed in custody of Keokuk, a rival Sauk friendly with Americans. Black Hawk dictated his autobiography in 1833 and then in 1837 Keokuk took him along on a second tour of the East. Black Hawk died the following summer. Many prominent men of the day defined their careers around Black Hawk. In some ways, so did Twain.

"Well den: we ain't got no Injuns, we doan' need no Injuns, en what does we want to go en hunt 'em up f'r? We's gitt'n along jes' as well as if we had a million un um. Dey's a powerful onery lot, anyway."

"Who is?"

"Why, de Injuns."

"Who says so."

"Why, I says so."

"What do you know about it?"

"What does I know 'bout it? I knows dis much. Ef dey ketches a body out, dey'll take en skin him same as dey would a dog. Dat's what I knows 'bout 'em."

"All fol-de-rol. Who told you that?"

"Why, I hear ole Missus say so."

"Ole Missus! The widow Douglas! Much she knows about it. Has she ever been skinned?"

"Course not."

"Just as I expected. She don't know what she's talking about. Has she ever been amongst the Injuns?"

"No."

"Well, then, what right has she got to be blackguarding them and telling what ain't so about them?"

"Well, anyway, ole Gin'l Gaines, he's ben amongst 'm, anyway."

"All right, so he has. Been with them lots of times hasn't he?"

"Yes—lots of times."

"Been with them years, hasn't he?"

"Yes sir! Why, Mars Tom, he—"

"Very well, then. Has he been skinned? You answer me that."[13]

The General Gaines that Twain refers to was hardly fictional. Major General Edmund P. Gaines (1777-1849) was a hero of the War of 1812 and soldiered for Andrew Jackson in campaigns against the Creek and Seminole. In 1831 General Gaines was commandant at Jefferson Barracks, near St. Louis. That year Gaines led a force of U.S. regulars north to Saukenuk at the request of William Clark, Superintendent of Indian Affairs. William Clark was youngest brother of George Rogers Clark and famous in his own right for having accompanied Merriwether Lewis to the Pacific West Coast. He wanted Gaines to remove Black Hawk and his band to the west side of the Mississippi. On arriving at Saukenuk, Gaines outlined the government's objectives, and his own. He reviewed the several treaties since 1804 that affirmed government purchase of Sauk tribal lands. Then he laid out his immediate objective, removal of Black Hawk's Band. At that point the council became quite heated. Black Hawk, and those treating with him, had entered Gaines' council chambers in full battle array. The warriors were painted and carried arms to show Gaines that they were not afraid. Black Hawk protested removal. Gaines, knowing Black Hawk had no civil authority within the tribe, taunted him. If he was ever close to being skinned, it was then. To Gaines' challenge Black Hawk replied,

> I will tell you who I am. I am a Sac; my father was a Sac; all the nations call me a SAC! I am a warrior, and so was my father. Ask those young men who have followed me to battle, and they will tell you who Black Hawk is; provoke me to war and you will learn who Black Hawk is.[14]

Gaines was unmoved. He gave the natives two days to leave Saukenuk. Sensing the general's resolve, Black Hawk abandoned the village at the last possible moment. With no natives to fight, some seven hundred disgruntled Illinois volunteers burned Saukenuk and its fields. The next day those militia were paroled back to their farms. Then Gaines called Black Hawk to council and made him sign a treaty that forbade return to the village. As compensation for the burned crops Gaines offered provisions, mostly corn. Thereafter the affair became known by wags as the Corn War. The next year, when Black Hawk returned again, so did the militia. That second year no quarter was offered.

Black Hawk was indeed a Sac. The complete name for the tribe was Osakiwug which translates as either, "People of the outlet" or "Yellow earth people." The Sac, more commonly known today as Sauk, were, since the time of earliest French records, allied with the Fox, Pottawatomi, Kickapoo, Mascouten, Winnebago and Miami. Collectively they were known as the "People of the Fire," or "Gens de Feu." Black Hawk was descended from the Thunder clan. In the opening pages of his autobiography he relates his traditional heritage. He traces lineage from his great-great grandfather, Mukataquet, through Nanamakee to his own father, Pyesa. His lineage intertwines with tribal heritage, a heritage embodied in the great medicine bag, the soul of the Sauk nation. At his surrender Black Hawk said this about the medicine bag:

> I told him it was the soul of the Sac nation—that it had never been dishonored in any battle—take it, it is my life— dearer than life.[15]

I could find no record of beliefs held in or represented by Sauk medicine bags. But I found something similar, the Owl Sacred Pack of the Fox Indians. The Fox, more properly the Mesquakie, were close allies of the Sauk and Black Hawk. Many followed him to defeat. They too were "People of the Fire" and believed in the power of medicine bags, or sacred packs. It is likely that the traditional Fox view of their sacred packs also held them to be dearer than life. I first read the Owl Sacred Pack in St. Louis' Mercantile Library. There, in the main reading room, oil portraits of Sauk and Fox chiefs and warriors, contemporaries of Black Hawk, hang above the shelves. Painted by George Catlin, the portraits are untitled. Those nameless men looked down on me as I read Owl Sacred Pack quoted at length below.

> Then (Owl said to them): "My grandchildren I bless you. There is nothing evil in the way I have thought of you. I have thought of you indeed in a good way. So long as your life shall endure, so long shall I make it go for you. And from time to time you will continue to gladden (the people) by what you do: such is the blessing I shall continue to bestow upon you. But my grandchildren, do not expect anything in return from your fellow people whom you have pleased. That is the only thing I tell you. And you will use my body, for I bless you, not any one. But it is not I alone. The one yonder who has power over your lives, is he who really plans this. This is what I tell you. I bless you as I tell you. He who is leading one blesses you. But you will always think of me. Do not throw me out of your thoughts. Verily I too have put my thought in here (the sacred pack) when I blessed you. When I think (of going) yonder, I go thither. I arrive at where I am going. Even if there were a river flowing by, I would come there; nothing would go wrong with me; even if there were a cliff where I was going I should go there. I would not be hindered at all. And you here, you would be hindered if there a river flowed by; you might seek a shallow spot, or you might make a boat if you crossed. You would not then come quickly: something would go wrong with you there. That is one way I bless you. If a river is deep and wide, you will wade easily across."[16]

However religious Black Hawk may have been, the medicine bag of the Sauk nation did not prevail amongst his followers at Battle Island, or afterwards. His people did not wade easily across. The few gaunt survivors of the massacre, nearly dead from starvation, attempted to reach Keokuk's villages in Iowa. For the one hundred or so who crossed the river, more violence awaited them. Wabasha, a Dakota chief, had been alerted by American officials to guard the river's western bank. He and his followers hunted down and killed sixty-eight of the refugees, capturing twenty-two others.

I stopped to rest at Battle Island the afternoon I left La Crosse. Nowadays it faces a county park named for Black Hawk. The island is just downstream from the Mississippi's first nuclear power plant at Genoa, Wisconsin. For economic reasons the plant burns coal now, though fissionable material continues to decay in the reactor's core. The unused power emanating from that bundle of uranium rods is a testament to obsolete science. Within sight of the plant, a marker commemorates the massacre at Battle Island. It, too, is a testament, in that place where so many "People of Fire" died.

> You have all witnessed the power which was given to me by the Great Spirit, in making that fire—and all that I now ask is...never let it go out...preserve peace among you, and administer to the wants of the needy: And should an enemy invade our country, I will then, but not until then, assume command, and go forth with my band of brave warriors, and endeavor to chastise them![17]

This injunction accompanied the great Sauk medicine bag as it passed from heir to heir. Black Hawk learned and believed the injunction. It is ironic how alike the Sauk language regarding their tribal medicine bag is to our present-day perception and language regarding a bundle of uranium rods.

Black Hawk, prior to the massacre, attempted to parley for peace a third time at the head of Battle Island. The two times previous, once before hostilities began and a second time after the war's first major engagement, he'd been unsuccessful. With his bedraggled band cornered at the Mississippi, Black Hawk realized his position was hopeless. He signaled truce to the *Warrior,* a steamboat armed with cannon, as it approached the island. Its captain, Joseph Throckmorton, was a man Black Hawk knew and trusted. The *Warrior* was returning downstream from having encouraged Wabasha to guard the river's west bank. When Black Hawk called to Throckmorton, the captain answered with a cannonade of grapeshot, opening the massacre.

They all crowded up and leaned over the rails, nearly in my face, and kept still, watching with all their might. I could see them first-rate, but they couldn't see me. Then the captain sung out: "Stand away!" and the canon left off such a blast right before me that it made me deef with the noise and pretty near blind with the smoke, and I judged I was gone. If they'd a had some bullets in, I reckon they'd a got the corpse they was after. Well, I see I warn't hurt, thanks to goodness.[18]

Twain's cannon shoots point blank at Huck, but it is empty, an ironic seeker of the dead. The dead it raises, the one remembered by the river at least, is Black Hawk. Huck lays concealed in a thicket on three-mile-long Jackson's Island, just down from a ferry landing. Twain introduced the island in an escapade involving Huck, Tom Sawyer and their bosom pal, Joe Harper. There is no such island near Hannibal, Missouri. But Twain, once a steamboat cub-pilot, was familiar with the river. Three-mile-long Jackson Island is just opposite Harper's Ferry, Iowa, twenty miles south of the Battle Island massacre. It's probable that Twain drew inspiration for his stories from facts he'd gathered along the river. If so, it appears that a good many of those facts may have been borrowed from Black Hawk's story. Huck's cannon fire is one and his hiding place is another. Black Hawk's autobiography recounts a similar incident:

During our stay in the thicket, a party of whites came close by us, but passed on without discovering us.[19]

The causes of Black Hawk's War are complex and numerous. Black Hawk and his followers were traditionalists. Corn, grown by women, was a staple in the Sauk diet. The tilled fields at Saukenuk were far more productive than unbroken prairie west of the Mississippi. The women did not want to leave their fields. One, a chief's daughter, pleaded with General Gaines that the Sauk be allowed to stay. He dismissed her by saying that the president had not sent him to make treaties with women.

But lead mines played the darkest role in bringing on Black Hawk's War. The area where Iowa, Wisconsin and Illinois join at the Mississippi was once rich in lead. Julien Dubuque began lead mining in 1788 at the site of the city named for him. In 1796 he was granted land rights there by Spanish officials, though the Fox tribe retained title. Potosi, his wife, was native, as were many of those who worked his mines. By his death in 1810, Sauk, Fox, and Iowa natives were mining lead throughout the region. That year alone, four hundred thousand pounds were produced between Prairie du Chien, Wisconsin and Rock Island, Illinois. Most of the metal was traded with the British in Canada, which irritated American officials at St. Louis. After Dubuque's death, title to his mines became a contentious issue. For a brief time, the Fox tribe held the upper hand.

In 1822 American officials opened the lead region east of the river to settlers. Immediately miners began staking claims previously worked by natives. Illinois miners were labeled "suckers" because they traveled north in the spring to work mines and south in the fall to escape winter—just like migrating suckers, a species of river fish. Wisconsin miners tended to dig in and hole up when winter came. They became known as "badgers". When the Sauk and Fox protested claim jumping to their agent, they were bullied west and told to work Dubuque's mines. But Iowa was dangerous for the Fox tribe. Their age-old enemies, the allied Sioux tribes of Dakota, Osage and Menomonee, roamed the area around Dubuque. Fox resettlement there led to conflict and bloodshed. William Clark convened a peace council at Prairie du Chien to settle tribal territories. This was the same Council of 1825 that set boundaries for the Sioux and Ojibwa in the north, near the Mississippi headwaters. That northern treaty created a buffer zone between the Sioux and Ojibwa, one that ultimately failed. In the south a similar buffer zone to separate the Sioux from the Sauk and Fox was created. It also failed.

In 1830 actions to transfer power in the lead region were begun in earnest. American officials called another council at Prairie du Chien. On the surface its premise was to settle disputes and make reparations between tribes, the Fox and Sioux. But there is evidence that a larger, more sinister strategy was in play. The Fox, those operating the Dubuque mines, set off to attend the peace council. Their deputation of prominent chiefs proceded upriver unarmed, as befits a peaceful delegation. While en route they were slaughtered by a war party of Sioux and Menomonee. The treachery lay in this: American officials had aided the Sioux war party.

> The following...is information that may be depended on, and will shew, that the Fox Chiefs and others of their nation were led into a snare that they little expected. Sometime in the month of April 1830 Captain Wyncoop Warner who was then Sub-Agent for the Fox Indians who resided at Dubuque's Mines, wrote me a letter...stating...that he had received a letter from

General Street Indian Agent at Prairie des Chiens, requesting him to get the Fox Chiefs...to meet the Sioux, Minnominie & Winnebagoe Indians for the purpose of making peace among them...there was...knowledge in that place about the War-party of Sioux and Minnominie Indians coming down the Mississippi to make war against the Fox Indians...I have reason to believe it was publicly known to the whole population of that place...You will see...that Mr. Taliaferro Indian Agent at St. Peters met the Sioux War-party on their way down... and give them ammunition, provision and Tobacco, they (the Sioux Indians) telling Mr. Taliaferro where they were going, and what to do, and he telling the Indians, they might do as they pleased...It has always been my opinion, that both General Street and Mr. Talliaferro ought to have been made to account for the evil doings in this case of fomenting the murdering of inoffensive Indians unarmed, and going on the invitation from Government Agents to make peace, but Genl Clark had his feelings or views in not representing to his Government the truth of that shameful affair.[20]

Thomas Forsyth, who wrote the above letter, was Indian Agent at Rock Island from 1819 until the Fox chiefs were murdered. Removed from office without cause, he learned later that rumors about him had circulated in Washington leading to his dismissal. He was alleged to have been a British agent during the War of 1812, a traitor. Forsyth suspected that William Clark, his old boss, had planted the rumors.

In 1831 Sauk and Fox warriors revenged the deaths of their chiefs on an encampment of drunken Menomonees. American officials demanded that the perpetrators be turned over. For the Sauk and Fox the demand seemed patently unjust. No such demand had been made of the Sioux. Unsurprisingly, the fugitives aligned themselves with Black Hawk. The final die was being cast. From Washington the tenor of the times was this:

But, alas! The Indians melt away before the white man, like snow before the sun! Well sir! Would you keep the snow and lose the sun! It is the order of nature we exclaim against. Jacob will forever obtain the inheritance of Esau. We cannot alter the law of Providence, as we read them in the experience of ages. The earth was given for labor, and to labor it belongs. The gift was not to the red, or to the white, but to the human race—and the inscription was, to the Wisest—the Bravest—to Virtue—and to Industry.[21]

President Jackson's views of natives were similar to those above. He wanted all tribesmen moved west of the Mississippi and their land claims in the east extinguished. Illinois' Governor Reynolds stepped to Washington's drum. He demanded removal of the Sauk and Fox from Rock Island, calling their presence there an invasion. Superintendent Clark, charged with removal, was in a delicate position. Clark wanted title for Dubuque's mines. He tried to buy the mines in a council held with the Fox after their chiefs were murdered. The natives refused his offer, demanding higher compensation. Clark needed some way to break the impasse, a way to control the negotiating process. When Black Hawk crossed into Illinois again in April 1832, Clark finally had the lever he needed. The army was alerted and all the machinery for war put in motion. Clark, like so many new Americans, was eager to get the lead out.

> *Well, the woman fell to talking about how hard times was, and how poor they had to live, and how the rats was free as if they owned the place, and so forth, and so on, and then I got easy again. She was right about the rats. You'd see one stick its nose out of a hole in the corner every little while. She said she had to have things handy to throw at them when she was alone, or they wouldn't give her no peace. She showed me a bar of lead, twisted up into a knot...I got the thing, and the first rat that showed his nose I let drive, and if he'd a stayed where he was he'd a been a tolerable sick rat.*[22]

In Twain's story the lump of lead was a contrivance the woman used to betray Huck's girlish disguise. Lead, in Black Hawk's story, also unveils betrayal.

I reached Dubuque on July 3rd, two days out from La Crosse. My landfall there was a tiny island just shy of the city's lock and dam. Motorboats were anchored randomly above the floodgates, waiting for Independence Day celebrations to begin. Groping my way through stinging nettles and mud I tried to find space on the island for my tent. Suddenly, three military helicopters came muttering over the dam in formation. In the half light of dusk their searchlights strafed the island. Almost immediately they were followed by a wing of fighter jets spilling white contrails. My holiday had begun.

After setting the tent I stretched out to watch Dubuque's fireworks from an old snag washed up in the shallows. Searchlights played the darkness from the top of Eagle Point, calling attention to the launching place. Meanwhile, a speedboat hove in and anchored nearby, within whispering distance. I tried to let the teenage couple know I was there, several times, but they were too busy. It'd be hard to say which pyrotechnics were most colorful, those on shore, or those onboard. When the fireworks ended I got up to leave the narrow snag. I wanted to go quietly but my legs were so stiff that I lost my footing. I backflopped into the muddy water with a tremendous splash. The woman in the boat was screaming when I sat up, but I was fine.

Next morning, July 4th, it seemed like all the boats from the night before were waiting with me at the lock. When our turn came and as the lock filled, my canoe seemed hopelessly small, fragile as an eggshell. As we all discharged, a forty-foot yacht three stories high almost capsized me. Its pilot let curiosity drive his boat right alongside my canoe. He asked where I was going. About the time he was ready for my answer his wake overran my gunwales, and poured about five inches of slosh for my feet to wade in. He stood at his bridge rail twenty feet above me apologizing profusely. Then he tried to patch things up by offering a Bloody Mary. It was obvious that the one in his hand hadn't been drawn from the morning's first batch. I was in for a long weekend.

South of Dubuque, at Tete Des Morts creek, I sheltered beneath a train trestle from a one-cloud rainstorm. A low blackness warned me into shore just before rain began falling in sheets. Lightning shivered the bluffs above, trying to find faults in the rock faces. Thunder rolled through the rain driving it forward on the wind. When the black cloud passed a double rainbow of intense colors fleeted across the river. Tete Des Morts, Head of the Dead, was named for skulls found there by French traders. A party of Sioux had been cornered and massacred in the salient where the creek enters the Mississippi at the foot of the bluffs. Black Hawk, recounting stories of his youth, remembered such a battle against the Sioux.

As I prepared to launch my canoe a hawk screeched from a dead tree over the river. His perch was a heavy limb well out from the bank. The tree was smooth and white as bone, its bark shed long ago. Bare of small branches, the tree hadn't leafed for more than a decade. Only the broken trunk and stubs of the larger limbs remained. Near its top the raptor strained forward at each piercing cry, wings akimbo, its plumage wet. Alone amongst the others this tree seemed very like a man.

The next night I took a hotel room in Bellevue, Iowa, a charming little mainstreet sort of town. The Inn there is a classic river tavern of the first order. Its rooms, bar and restaurant all evoke the era Twain made famous in his stories. The barroom was raucous and bawdy with celebration of the holiday. Two Chicago comedians tried the crowd and were well received. By the time I settled over a catfish dinner at the bar, the first act was over. The second, a woman named Marge Takes, would have made Twain's Royal Nonesuch Players blanche. Her routine hinged on criticism of porno films. She compared flaws in their characters, plots, dialogue and camera angles. Her monologue was paced with expletives. The punch line, which never failed to bring down the house, was always the same. "Shut the F——- UP!" The catfish was delicious.

The woman down from me at the bar was cousin to one of the bartenders. They were celebrating their shared July 5th birthday. She was twenty-one, legally drinking for the first time and enthralled by the show. He was several years older and a good deal more sober. Also present were a couple of engineers who together had invented the one-and-a-half gallon toilet. Old model toilets use seven gallons of water. All we patrons agreed that the invention was a very good thing. Our motto was, "Less water for sewers and more for the brewers." But it was too much for our neophyte reveler. She had to be taken home by one of the engineers. His invention would have been no use to the young woman. She became incontinent in her parents' front yard.

Black Hawk claimed to know the value of temperance.

> I visited all the whites and begged them not to sell whisky to my people. One of them continued the practise openly. I took a party of my young men, went to his house, and took the barrel and broke in the head and turned out the whisky.[23]

In his last years though, Black Hawk was said to have tippled brandy in steamboat bar rooms. Twain, on the other hand, didn't hold much tolerance in temperance or those who talked it. He made Injun Joe bear the brunt of his indignation.

> "I didn't see anything but a bottle and a tin cup on the floor by Injun Joe; yes, and I saw two barrels and lots more bottles in the room. Don't you see, now, what's the matter with that ha'nted room?"
> "How?"

"Why it's ha'nted with whisky! Maybe all the Temperance Taverns have got a ha'nted room, hey Huck?"[24]

Two days south of Bellevue, just above Davenport, Iowa, I met some of the people Marge Takes ridicules, the porno stars. It was late afternoon on the last day of the long holiday weekend. My charts showed Steamboat Island to be the last likely camp above the Quad Cities. When I arrived there a group in bathing suits was lounging on the island's small beach. Others of their party were water-skiing on the main channel. As I approached one of the men muttered something unflattering about my appearance. Undeterred, I asked if I could land anyway and that same man waved me in. The bathers were all young and remarkably good looking. It soon became obvious that they had laid claim for the day to this side of the island. The main channel side, however, was considered public domain. This near side was a campsite complete with beach, fire ring, table and a makeshift toilet. The other side consisted of a place to moor boats and a rope swing.

While I dragged my canoe up the beach the ski boat circled past and dropped its skier. Specially designed for pulling, the boat rode low in the water. The driver finished his loop and cut the big inboard to an idle, drifting down from the head of the island. He was perhaps twenty years older than the others and not nearly so fit. His bow was pointed toward the beach and my canoe. Looking directly at me, he asked who wanted to ski next. Then, without waiting for reply, he gunned the boat onto shore. It stopped only inches from my feet.

At the same time, on the other side of the island, an Army Corps of Engineers vessel pulled in beneath the rope swing. Its captain ordered a young man in the tree to drop the rope swing and climb down. A uniformed crewman in an orange lifevest, terribly overdressed for the island, clambered from the vessel onto the bank. The ski boat driver, still looking at me, asked again who wanted to ski. A woman seated behind him said simply, "Take me home." With that cue the driver broke his glare and I started pulling my duffel out of the canoe. The ski boat was pushed back into the channel and roared off toward LeClaire, Iowa, the nearest landing. Those of us still on the island became involved in the rope swing drama. On this last day of the holiday, the captain had been given orders to remove rope swings because they were public hazards. Armed with pruning shears his crewman began climbing the launch tree, then severed the rope swing. The captain reasoned for our benefit that the hawser had probably been stolen from the Corps in the first place. That said, the Corps left the island taking along the rope's knotted end. In less than ten minutes there was another scavenged length of rope being knotted onto the swing's remainder. The launch tree was back in business and Steamboat Island was once again attracting swingers.

My reluctant island hosts invited me to choice of a beer or soda. From their conversations I learned that the ski boat driver made porno films in his home. Though he lived mostly alone, they were all welcome to his parties. His sister was among those on the island. She called his house a brothel. I gathered that his boat was a recruiting tool. No one on the island knew the woman he'd taken back to LeClaire. When the driver returned the others boarded for a slow drift back to the Quad Cities. From mid-channel he hollered, "Look us up when you get in town." That night as stars began to appear and reflect on the water I marveled at how still the river was. I looked downstream, to where I had never been. I thought about the LeClaire woman's request, a command really. Its simplicity had made it irresistible, "Take me home."

Antoine LeClaire was the interpreter who translated Black Hawk's autobiography from Sauk to English. He was also interpreter for the Sauk and Fox in council negotiations and was given lands by the natives for his services. With those lands he became co-founder of Davenport, Iowa and grew wealthy. That did not keep him from being the butt of Sauk jokes, however. LeClaire, a rotund man, accompanied Black Hawk during his second tour of the East in 1837. When curious onlookers would inquire which of the natives was the famous warrior:

> Sauk pranksters amused themselves by pointing to the interpreter Antoine LeClaire, a balloon-shaped man, so obese he could hardly move. The joke always moved LeClaire to a paroxysm of rage, while Black Hawk sat completely impassive and immobile.[25]

The town of LeClaire, Iowa is at the head of what used to be an upper set of rapids bracketing Rock Island. During the steamboat era the town was home for pilots who specialized in navigating that most dangerous section of river. Roustabouts would wait beneath a big elm there known as the Green Tree. One of the river's last working steam paddlewheelers is on blocks in LeClaire as a museum attraction. At the local diner I was introduced to a collector of steamboat memorabilia, a man famous amongst steamboat aficionados. We spent a very enjoyable evening looking at his collection and talking. When I asked if he knew anything of the area's natives he brought out a newspaper article featuring a picture of his son. Digging in the yard one spring his son had found human bones and some arrow points. After contacting authorities, the bones were turned over to the Fox tribe at Tama, Iowa for reburial. The boy was disappointed at not being allowed to participate in the natives' ceremony. Since that spring my host has discovered other native graves on his lot, but he no longer seeks publicity. He's since learned that his property could be designated a burial ground and his lot would become worthless. Nowadays native burial grounds are prohibitively expensive for new construction. It was not so in Black Hawk's time.

Black Hawk returned to Saukenuk in the spring of 1830 to find that the government had sold the village. The buyer was George Davenport, a trader with the Sauk and Fox, supposedly their friend. His purchase of three thousand acres included the village proper, most of its surrounding fields and the burial grounds. Davenport had been a trader in the area since 1816 and knew how to get things done. In 1831, the year of eviction, he collected tribal annuities of some $8,000, with rights to more.

> *That made me feel pretty bad. About an hour or two ago, it would a been a little different, but now it made me feel bad and disappointed. The king rips out and says: "What! And not sell out the rest o' the property? March off like a passel o' fools and leave eight or nine thousand dollars worth o' property layin' around jest sufferin' to be scooped in?—and all good saleable stuff, too.'"*
> *The duke he grumbled; said the bag of gold was enough, and he didn't want to go no deeper—didn't want to rob a lot of orphans of everything they had.*[26]

Davenport was murdered in his own bed on July 4, 1845. His wife found him there covered in blood, at the point of death. She was his second wife and by that point Davenport was a respected man in the community. He'd been made colonel in the Illinois militia and had a new home on Rock Island, overlooking the rapids. His wife had been feted in Davenport's absence at Independence celebrations held across the river. George, feeling poorly, had stayed home. His wife had double reason to mourn Davenport's passing: George was both her husband and her father.

Davenport's murderers were river bandits, thought to be part of a gang operating out of Nauvoo, Illinois. The gang was known as the "Banditti of the Prairie," an appellation and history disputed yet today by the Mormon Church. It seems the Mormons were a law unto themselves for a while. Until May of 1845 they held municipal court powers in Nauvoo, Illinois. That court took precedence over state courts and was sometimes requested as venue by accused thieves. Tithing to the Mormon Church was thought to earn a sympathetic ear in Nauvoo's courts. How goods for tithing were obtained was thought to matter somewhat less. When Nauvoo was lost as a judicial haven the Banditti dispersed and there was an upwelling of the underworld all along the river. George Davenport is thought to have been only one of the victims.

I toured Rock Island on my bicycle. Its modern name is Arsenal Island for the installation commissioned there under the influence of Governor Reynolds after Black Hawk's War. The Rock Island Arsenal replaces what had been the Sauk's playground.

> We did not, however, object to their building the fort on the island, but we were very sorry, as this was the best island on the Mississippi, and had long been the resort of our young people during the summer. It was our garden (like the white people have near to their big villages) which supplied us with strawberries, blackberries, gooseberries, plums, apples, and nuts of different kinds; and its waters supplied us with fine fish, being situated in the rapids of the river. In my early life, I spent many happy days on this island. A good spirit had care of it, who lived in a cave in the rocks immediately under the place where the fort now stands, and has often been seen by our people. He was white, with large wings like a swan's, but ten times larger. We were particular not to make much noise in that part of the island which he inhabited, for fear of disturbing him. But the noise of the fort has since driven him away, and no doubt a bad spirit has taken his place![27]

Nowadays a tank guards Arsenal Island at the bridge connecting with the mainland. Tagged lots of gun barrel stock for howitzers and field artillery rust in piles strewn along the island's south end. The swan's cave was long ago dynamited out of existence.

For many reasons it is easy to romanticize Black Hawk. In his lifetime he fought against William H. Harrison at Fort Meigs in Sanduskey, Ohio. He routed Zachary Taylor in a skirmish at Credit Island, where the Rock River enters the Mississippi. Abraham Lincoln was a captain in the Illinois militia that chased Black Hawk to Battle Island. Black Hawk was presented with a sword and a medal by Andrew Jackson.

John Quincy Adams also presented Black Hawk with a medal. Jefferson Davis escorted the old warrior from Prairie du Chien to St. Louis after his surrender. All those men were presidents, Davis in secession. They were leaders of their people in their time. They recognized Black Hawk as no less.

I was fifty miles south of Rock Island on July 11th, near Keithsburg, Illinois. That morning dawned soggy and grew steadily more dreary. After making oatmeal for breakfast I broke camp and set about dragging my canoe off the sand dune, back to another day of paddling. I wore an army surplus poncho, a swimming suit and sandals, looking I'm sure like a riverine Bedouin. Air trapped beneath the hooded poncho billowed warm gusts round my face with each paddlestroke. The moist air fogged and bespeckled my lenses until I couldn't see. I took the glasses off, and became part of the misty, watery world around me. The sky, an immense cushion of wetness, closed over the vale to speak a language of rain. Drops impacted the river, lifting tiny water stems in backsplash response. I saw patterns on the river where the rain fell, sinuous shadows limned by currents and countercurrents. I knew how much of me was water then, a plumped skinful of osmotic dust struggling with the world's diffusion. Around me, the banks hardly visible, all the earth seemed condensed to flowing river. Everything seemed made of water.

Downstream a sodden mirage of horizon began to grow solid and emerge. My charts read, "Trans-Action Railroad (Abandoned)." A thin black line levitated over the river from bank to island to bank. It was a bridge, extending from Iowa to Black Hawk Island to Illinois. Gradually, its intervals of quarried pilings become clear and then its hatchwork of rails and crossties. Over the main channel a section was missing. Left of the gap a huge concrete deadweight squatted over the pilings, enmeshed in a collapse of beams. Girders from its cantilever reached over the channel. They were all twisted off and broken, like a handful of amputated fingers. Then, scrimming toward me through the opening, I saw the *Mississippi Queen*.

The paddlewheeler's two black smokestacks jutted the sky like stovepipe hats from the last century. They advanced silently, an equation of barristers escorting the *Queen*. Rain stopped and the river lay quiet. This machine had come from another era, some dolorous bella donna untimed by the fog. Her forward decks were bunted in red, white and blue for the Independence holiday. As the *Queen* and I drew broadside one another, passengers braved saturating weather to come on deck with cameras. They clicked away at me and I at them. Barge pilots had taught me a bit of cordiality for encounters like these, a crossed-arms, full-sweep, river greeting. But few on board the *Queen* acknowledged. She was silent and the fog made the boat look pale. Her passage might have been an imagining were it not for her wake, the highest of any boat on the Mississippi. The wake was trailed by successively smaller waves. They lapped my hull like tenebrous hoofbeats of a departing carriage.

I stopped at Keithsburg for coffee and to wait out the rain which had returned in torrents. From a riverside campground I phoned my father to wish him a happy 64th birthday. Born 7-11-27, he has always considered his birthdate auspicious and himself lucky. Dad was well and in a good mood so we talked for quite a while. I told him I'd seen the *Mississippi Queen* that morning; he told me about some fish he'd caught. There was a partial eclipse in progress so I called Dad old Chief Hole-in-the-Day, hinting at the overlap of birthday and eclipse. He responded with a silence that said "round-the-bend." I'd mentioned the Ojibwa chief in earlier conversations, but Dad had forgotten. Neither was he paying any mind to his birthday's eclipse.

The payphone I used was mounted to an outdoor toilet's cinder block wall, within yards of the river. A curtain of rainwater arched from the roof eaves overhead to splash at my feet before champing down the asphalt boatramp. Nearby stood a fifty-gallon drum crudely lettered "Trash." Its fish stench was barely diluted by the rain. I pictured my father at his desk, talking with me. I thought of the dry, sweet, cleanness of his office, the crisp feel of his pressed cotton shirt and smooth-knotted silk tie. I realized that I couldn't much know how he felt that day, except about me. He couldn't have known much how I felt either, except about him. When I told him "good-bye" and "happy birthday," my father simply said, "Be careful."

Afterwards, over coffee, I learned from an old local that Keithsburg was known as Yellow Banks to the Sauk and Fox. Black Hawk had crossed the river there in April 1832, precipitating the Black Hawk War. How differently Black Hawk's War had begun from the Minnesota Conflicts thirty years later. There was no murder, kidnapping, harangue or all-night council to begin Black Hawk's War. The loudest noise may have been a paddle dip audible only to its maker. If there were any words, they were not spoken in a close-quartered cabin, or wickiup, but against the immense and perfect indifference of the river. Still, Black Hawk and Minnesota's dynasties are related: by the river, by cause, by participants and by outcome. Of perhaps fifteen hundred natives who followed Black Hawk across the river, nearly one thousand died. In treaties that ended the war, the Sauk and Fox tribes were permanently removed from Illinois. They were forced to concede lands in Iowa as well, including the Dubuque mines. Today the Fox, more properly the Mesquakie, have a small settlement near Tama, Iowa while the Sauk tribe is widely dispersed.

In the Cattermole Library of Fort Madison, Iowa an oil portrait of Black Hawk hangs above the fireplace in one of the reading rooms. Fort Madison is seventy miles above Hannibal, Missouri, near Black Hawk's last home. The fort, built in 1808, was abandoned and burned after Black Hawk's attack in 1811. It was his earliest and perhaps greatest triumph over the Americans. The Cattermole painting was commissioned by a man who had fallen in love with Black Hawk's daughter. The man intended to marry her but was ultimately dissuaded for fear of becoming a "Squaw Man." Fisher, the artist, never saw Black Hawk, painting instead from a life sketch supplied by the timorous suitor. Black Hawk is portrayed in his last years, long after the massacre at Battle Island. He is profiled in a frock coat with a high collar. A ruffled shirt and broad tie fan out between lapels above the coat's two brass buttons. Black Hawk's high, domed head is balded in front. His hair, thin and greying, is combed straight back and down, draping just over his collar. He hardly appears native, though black beads suspend from the top of his ear lobe. A red trade blanket, added like an afterthought of color, folds behind his shoulders.

Black Hawk died of a fever on Devil's Creek near Fort Madison in 1838. But his body doesn't rest there. In death, too, Twain spun Black Hawk's story into ironic fiction. Twain's native, Injun Joe, is portrayed as a grave robber working for a physician.

> *Potter and Injun Joe were carrying a handbarrow with a rope and a couple of shovels on it. They cast down their load and began to open the grave. The doctor put the lantern at the head of the grave and came and sat down with his back against one of the elm trees.*[28]

The historical reality is almost perfectly reversed. In reality it was Black Hawk's grave that was robbed and it was a physician who did it. A woman in Fort Madison told me the local legend, that Black Hawk's corpse was scalded in a hog kettle to remove the flesh and that his bones were exhibited in Pawnee Bill's Wild West Show. She was not far off. Black Hawk had been interred according to traditional Sauk custom. His body was placed on the earth in a sitting position, facing southeast, with his back supported by a wooden slab. He was wrapped in blankets with his medals, swords and other honoraria at hand. A log hut was built around him and sodded over with blue grass. A tribal totem was erected outside the hut and a twenty- foot sapling flew the American flag. Traditional articles of clothing, food and wampum sufficient for a three-day journey were interred as well. These supplies were to provision him on his journey to the spirit world. But the grave was violated. Within nine months of Black Hawk's burial Dr. James Turner stole the corpse, scalded it and had the bones wired together for exhibition. He planned to take Black Hawk back east. Turner was foiled when Iowa's Governor had the bones brought to Burlington and placed in an office near the Geological and Historical Institute for safekeeping.

Again, Twain's words are ironic. In this case, the eulogy with which Injun Joe is laid to rest:

> *The poor unfortunate had starved to death. In one place near at hand a stalagmite had been growing slowly up from the ground for ages, builded by the water-drip from a stalactite overhead. The captive had broken off the stalagmite, and upon the stump had placed a stone, wherein he had scooped a shallow hollow to catch the precious drop that fell once in every three minutes with the weary regularity of a clock-tick—a dessert spoonful once in every four and twenty hours. That drop was falling when the Pyramids were new; when Troy fell; when the foundations of Rome were laid; when Christ was crucified; when the Conqueror created the British empire; when Columbus sailed; when the massacre at Lexington was 'news.' It is falling now; it will still be falling when all these things shall have sunk down the afternoon of history, and the twilight of tradition, and been swallowed up in the thick night of oblivion. Has everything a purpose and a mission? Did this drop fall patiently during five thousand years to be ready for this flitting human insect's need? and has it another important object to accomplish ten thousand years to come? No matter. It is many and many a year since the hapless half-breed scooped out the stone to catch the priceless drops, but to this day the tourist stares longest at that pathetic stone and that slow dropping water when he comes to visit the wonders of McDougal's cave. Injun Joe's cup stands first in the list of the cavern's marvels; even "Alladin's Palace" cannot rival it. Injun Joe was buried near the mouth of the cave.*[29]

Twain makes Injun Joe's carved stone into a chalice and the cave into a cathedral. He buried the native with commentary befitting a bishop. The irony is that throughout the preceding story Injun Joe embodied horror, fear, suspense and violence. Those same elements were once popularly associated with Black Hawk. The greater irony is that while history has rescued Black Hawk from those associations, Twain's Injun Joe stereotype survives.

This chapter began with a quote from "Tom and Huck Amongst the Indians," a story that Twain never finished. Whatever his intentions, certain conclusions are inescapable. Twain and Black Hawk led proximate lives insofar as locale and era. Also, there are parallels in Twain's stories and Black Hawk's history too close for mere coincidence to explain. Whether Twain used Black Hawk for a pattern hardly matters against the clock-tick of a water drop. Still, part of Tom's long soliloquy fits partic'lar well right here.

> *Death?—an Injun don't care shucks for death. They prefer it. They sing when they're dying—sing their deathsong. You take an Injun and stick him full of arrows and splinters, and hack him up with a hatchet, and skin him, and start a slow fire under him, and do you reckon he minds it? No sir; he will just set there in the hot ashes, perfectly comfortable, and sing, same as if he was on salary.*[30]

The last refrain of this chapter belongs to Black Hawk. His story is the river's truest one, and anyway older than Twain's fiction. In 1855 the Burlington Geological and Historical Institute burned to the ground. Black Hawk's remains, housed in offices next door, went up in flames, too. Every trace of his wired skeleton was consumed. All earthly evidence of the warrior who'd led the "People of Fire" was gone.

Peace Medals

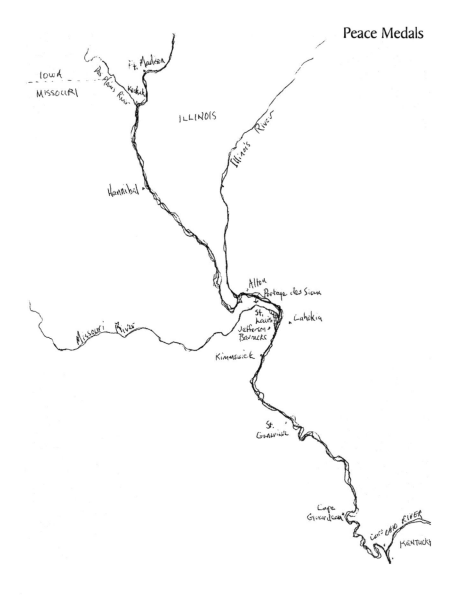

IOWA
MISSOURI
Des Plaines River
Ft. Madison
Keokuk
ILLINOIS
Illinois River
Hannibal
Alton
Portage des Sioux
St. Louis
Cahokia
Jefferson Barracks
Missouri River
Kimmswick
St. Genevieve
Cape Girardeau
Cairo OHIO RIVER
KENTUCKY

Peace Medals

It's 1:30 a.m. Sunday, July 13, 1991 in Fort Madison, Iowa. I am nine hundred and fifty miles downstream from the river's source, aboard a floating casino. I watch as gamblers file down the *Emerald Lady's* gangplank to its attendant barge, *The Jackpot*. Tonight's players seem well pleased. They saunter away as though in revue. Some are dressed in fine clothes bespeaking wealth, but most wear an assemblage of denim, the Midwest's compliant chic. Chance's addicts are not obvious here, the casino is too new. Close behind the gamblers follows their money, transformed into tokens. Sealed in duffels overwrapped with plastic bags, the bundled scrip is clumsy. Guards, themselves overwrapped in polyester, toddle it down the ramp. They, too, are sealed. Round their ample middles are wide black belts and on each one's breast a numbered badge.

I am three decks above, watching from the darkened pilothouse. Before me lays the river and a little beyond, a railroad bridge. Inside the pilothouse and within easy grasp are the vessel's controls. Though the instrument lights are very dim I can read the silkscreened labels: compass, rudder, throttles, bow thruster, searchlight, deck lights, engine clutch, calliope cutout, fire doors release, radar, sonar, swingmaster, engine temperature and fluid indicators, pump controls, stack release, rudder angle, and since this is a paddlewheeler, a control for that, too. Mounted beside the desk-large panel are a cellular phone, several radios and a fax machine.

Ben Rodgers, my pilot host, is gone below to the boiler deck with the engineer. At twenty-five, he is one of the youngest pilots on the river. He earned sea legs by piloting his parents' car ferry the single river mile between Nauvoo, Illinois and Commerce, Iowa. His parents, Daryl and Marcie, are on their third towboat now, the *Gadfly*. All summer long they cross and recross the Mississippi over the Mormons' path of westward exodus. Many of the Rodgers' passengers are Latter Day Saints retracing their ancestors' pilgrimage from Nauvoo. Dusty Utah license plates betray the pilgrims' home. On those odd days when their paths cross, the *Gadfly* never fails to sound its horn to the *Emerald Lady*. The greeting seems lewd from a boat numbered full with saints. Few passengers on either vessel know that the Rodgers are calling to their son.

Security has sealed off the Texas deck below while the slots are serviced. Returned now from scrip delivery, the guards are unaware of the prodigious mayfly hatch swarming aboard the hurricane deck. But I, from my vantage in the pilothouse, can see a marker light beginning to smolder beneath the railing. The marker's lens has broken and heat from its unprotected bulb is burning an attracted mass of flies. Legion others of the insect horde present themselves on the windows before me, wings folded neatly upwards like hands in prayer. Dawn will find the flies positioned as they are now, but stiffened and lifeless. The first morning wind will begin sweeping them into drifts and corner piles. Upriver they called them "fishflies," but here they're known as "mormonflies."

Guns and Roses burbles into this dimness sporadically interrupted by the marine radio. A barge pilot trades breaks with Fort Madison's swing bridge, the largest in the world. The bridge swings two railroad tracks and U.S. Highway 61 in lengthwise and crosswise pivot to the river. The bridge regulates the flow of trains, cars, trucks and towboats like a giant transistor of the globe's commerce. It is controlled from a windowed tower above the pivot. There the bridge master is holding off a southbound tow. Conversing with the tow's pilot, the master's radio protocol is clipped and definite as the bridge itself. He has closed the bridge for an eastbound Santa Fe freight, a hotshot. The train's engineer must have parleyed for priority on a radio band unmonitored aboard the *Emerald Lady*. For me the engineer's request is only hearsay. Looking west over Fort Madison's narrow band of city lights there is much blackness. The train, for now, is just a promise.

A third radio channel, crudely familiar, opens with this: "Hey George, are you there?" Over the walkie-talkie a slot attendant requests a mechanic from *The Jackpot*. One of the machines and its problem, a stiff lock, are specified by a unit number. The machines' alluring gambling names are unimportant now, meaningless to their efficient handlers. I turn off the AM radio and cross to the captain's couch. Kneeling into deep leather cushions I search the downstream night for the river. Toward the south, my constant heading, I see empty cocktail tables, insects, the smoldering lamp, and more darkness.

Gambling boats are the river's newest craze. The summer of my journey, Iowa was the first state to have them. But not for long. Illinois had passed enabling legislation and all nine other river states were considering it. Gambling boats attract people to the river, which is a good thing. Not since packet boats declined in favor of railroads have Iowa's river towns seen so many people. At season's peak two thousand passengers a week were riding the *Emerald Lady*. Unfortunately, chance is what draws the gamblers to the river. The river itself is only an excuse, an expedient. In the quirky flow of politics and profits the romance of the river is simply pretence.

Passengers on the *Emerald Lady* had cruised downstream to Keokuk, Iowa. There, had they been very aware, they might have seen Chief Keokuk's statue between the slots and beyond the windows. It stands atop a bluff at the summit of Grand Avenue, facing east across the river. The figure wears a feathered bonnet, though Catlin in painting three portraits of the chief never showed him so. Known for his peaceful endeavors, Keokuk holds a pipe in his right hand. Yet an attached plaque quotes him exhorting his people to war. It's as though Keokuk's statue had been inadvertently cast in Black Hawk's mold. Real life often found them at odds on tribal matters, on different sides of the same coin. Each was the likely outcome of the other—heads and tails, peace and war. Keokuk's statue stands as a contradiction. He and his tribe were removed from the very place that honors him. His monument is like the flashing lights above slot machines. They imply that chance favors the heavy player. Keokuk's monument implies that peace is won by practising war. History, like an oddsmaker for the house, knows better.

> The Indians were greatly addicted to gambling. Those who had contact with the British gambled with regular playing cards. They would stake their rations, their pelts, rifles, dogs, and sometimes even their squaws on the issue of a game. The Indians of the Missouri River clung to their native games. They gambled with a circular parchment box with a bottom shaped like a small drum. Out of this box they would cast

up in the air a number of small shells or pebbles, waving the palms of their hands horizontally between the falling pebbles and the box, and at the same time blowing upon the pebbles with their mouths.[31]

The scene above describes Portage des Sioux, Missouri, just upriver from St. Louis, in the summer of 1815. Thousands of natives were gathered there to conclude peace between tribes and the U.S. following the War of 1812. It was the most important native peace convocation of its day, and the largest ever held on the river. But not all the river's important native leaders attended. The dynastic chiefs, Wabasha, Little Crow, Decorah and Winneshiek, are not listed among the signers. No one from the Ojibwa tribe came. At first Black Hawk, too, refused to attend, though his absence was less surprising. He was absent because his village, Saukenuk, had been sold in an earlier treaty at Portage des Sioux. Black Hawk recognized neither the treaty nor its American negotiators. The Americans were persistent, however. They used a carrot and stick approach to attract tribes to the council, some $30,000 worth of gifts: "blankets, strouds, cloth, calicoes, glasses, knives, fire steels, rifles, fusils, flints, powder, tobacco, pipes, needles and etc." [Fisher] were distributed to the attendees. For those unattracted to largesse, like Black Hawk, force was used. Fort Armstrong was built at Rock Island to persuade the Sauk tribe to sign a Portage des Sioux treaty. Black Hawk signed, but his rival, Keokuk, did not. Perhaps in 1816 Keokuk was still too young to appreciate how peace is made.

Portage des Sioux is situated opposite and below the Illinois River's confluence with the Mississippi. Twenty miles downstream the Mississippi makes confluence again, with the Missouri. Overland between those two great rivers was a native shortcut from which the village takes its name, Portage des Sioux. The two mile portage allowed natives to transgress some forty miles of river. During floods the rivers make portages of their own. The low banks of the village and the level fields behind it have frequently been inundated. The town, like so many on the Mississippi, time-drifts. It is spare, compact and quiet. Floods are its crises, each one laying down new strata of history, or washing it away. The town seems more an accretion of river drift than of people.

I learned of the council held at Portage des Sioux from an inscribed boulder lying on its side beneath the town's water tower. By both position and message the boulder could have been detritus tumbled into the village by high water. It read "Indian Treaties 1815-1925," nothing more. The year 1925 had nothing to do with the treaties; it simply dates the monument. I found the curious marker while bicycling into town. My destination was Portage des Sioux's leading tourist attraction, Our Lady of the Rivers shrine. On the concrete pier leading to the shrine I found another, more informative council monument. A decorative abutment there says, "1815 Treaty between all warring Indian tribes and the U.S. signed at Portage des Sioux. In 1815 representatives of Indian tribes arrived in several thousand canoes to negotiate a peace treaty with the white settlers." Impressed by its message I leaned my bike against the abutment and walked toward the shrine.

As I walked I imagined thousands of canoes making landfall. I imagined native emissaries, standing forward, braced, prepared to leave their ribbed, birchbark hollows. How beautiful the river must have been then, lined with canoes and bustling with activity. The treaty visitors talked, gambled, traded, smoked and played ball games. They painted and bedecked themselves with feathers, beads, furs and blankets. One Omaha chieftain wore a buffalo robe depicting the Missouri flowing through a series of hands, black and red. The black hands represented his people and red hands places where they had been attacked and killed. As tribal emissary, the chief talked in council using his robe as a storyboard in the presence of both allies and enemies. Over twenty tribes shared a common camp space and talked at Portage des Sioux. The council was a time of peace. But it was also a time of tension and vulnerability. Walking the pier at Portage des Sioux I could almost smell fear in the air from those many years ago. A little later I realized it wasn't fear, but emissions. A nearby power plant was tainting the sky with sulphur.

The view from Portage des Sioux's shrine is unobstructed across the Mississippi to Illinois. Tree-shrouded limestone rock-faces rise from the river there, perhaps one hundred feet high, vertically cupped by erosion. The even formation of indents and projections are known as the Illinois Palisades. Looking across to them I marveled at their sculpted regularity and thought of the river, giant and swirling, that had formed them eons ago. My own paddle swirls were puny by comparison. Thousands and millions of them together could not begin such a record. The shrine, a stylized white Madonna, faces those Palisades. Its fiberglass form was raised after Mary's intercession during the flood of 1951. In 1973 another, deeper flood inundated the village. Waters rose to the top of the Madonna's pedestal. Since then the statue has become more a symbol of peace than of flood prevention.

The council at Portage des Sioux is relatively unimportant by today's historical standards. Its only stated purpose was to formalize peace between various tribes and the U.S. government. No land was sold, nor prisoners exchanged. It was still pretty early on the Western frontier. Portage des Sioux council invitations were distributed to tribes all along the Illinois, Mississippi and Missouri valleys. In total, thirty-seven tribes were invited. But only half that many signed treaties. The disparity shows how uncertain officials were in identifying native tribes. The U.S. frontier was so vast and unfamiliar that administrators simply did not know who lived where.

Before beginning my trip I sent out invitations, too. I contacted every major newspaper on the Mississippi hoping to write and sell a serialized account of my journey. The response was underwhelming. Apparently newspapers do not buy freelance adventure journalism from amateurs. There was one exception, an enthusiastic phone call from Mr. Gene Liss at *Limelight Magazine*. *Limelight* is a black society monthly in St. Louis. The paper prints feature stories, presumably those of interest to its readers. I can't imagine St. Louis' black community was much interested in a middle-aged white man canoeing down the river. But Gene Liss, the editor, is an avid sports enthusiast and an arts impresario. He bought my series.

Portage des Sioux is an old town. It is first recorded as an unnamed village of the Tamaroa Indians. Father Hennepin rested with the Tamaroa before journeying up the Mississippi in 1680. A Spanish fort built in 1799 initiated the town's military role. By then, unlicensed French fur traders had already made it a popular exchange post. Following the Louisiana Purchase in 1803, frontier expeditions sought last minute supplies at the village. Merriwether Lewis and William Clark drew men and goods from Portage des Sioux before their epic journey to the Pacific. During the War of 1812 General Howard assembled Missouri's nascent militia at Portage des Sioux prior to his campaign up the Illinois River. Portage des Sioux was a convenient location in frontier days. Proximate to three major rivers, it was also comfortably distant from the vices of St. Louis.

William Clark, already U.S. territorial governor of Missouri, was appointed by President Monroe to make peace with natives following the War of 1812. Also appointed as "commissioners pleniopotentiary" were Ninian Edwards, territorial governor of Illinois, and Auguste Chouteau. Chouteau, one of St. Louis' founders, was a wealthy fur trader. His influence extended far and wide, notably on the Mississippi. Clark, by virtue of his explorations, was familiar with tribes of the Missouri while Edwards was superintendent for tribes on the Illinois.

In many ways the council of Portage des Sioux was a naming function. The treaties were negotiated in common and treaty language was in each case identical. Only the tribal names were different. Subsequent treaties negotiated with several tribes or singly were, by contrast, each one unique. They concerned tribal boundaries. Still later rounds of the treaty process "extinguished" native land claims. Thus, the naming function was of primary importance. Whether pretext or impetus, peace treaties placed tribes under U.S. dominion. They named native peoples into manageable units. It was no small task in 1815. Consider, as one measure of its immensity, names of the Kansa tribe.

> I've come across 140 ways to spell Kansas, and...I've found 171 variations...Kansa and its forms have been translated as wind, windy, wind people, south wind people, those-who-come-like-wind-across-the-prairie, swift, swift wind, swift river, swift water, smoky water, fire people, plum people...
>
> Six full-blood Kansa, all men and all but one over sixty-five, are still living but none of them can speak more than a few words of the old language; they use almost exclusively the word Kaw for the tribe even though they know their parents called themselves Konsay...(they) accept "people of the South Wind" or "Wind People" as the meaning of the name.[32]

When Clark and the other commissioners named the tribes at Portage des Sioux they were literally trying to capture the wind.

Native tribes on the U.S. frontier were mobile and their alliances fluid. They defined themselves as much by relationship as by name. Individuals were also grouped into families, known as gens, which transcended tribal lines. Thus, the Osage, Omaha and Kansa tribes all had gens named Honga whose totem was an eagle. Europeans, in naming tribes, sometimes confused gens and tribal names. The Fox tribe is a case in point. The first French contact with the tribe met members of the Fox gens. Though their tribal name was Meshkwakihug, the Red Earth People, the French named them and so history knows them, as the Fox. Like the French, Clark and the commissioners condensed intricacies of idiom, seasonal migration, tribal structure and family totems to simple written names. It was like naming a tree by describing its trunk.

The confusion of tribal names devolved to individuals as well. Personal naming customs, dynamic and peculiar to each tribe, did not fit European convention. The names of chiefs might be titular, personal, or dynastic, such as those of Minnesota's Dakota. Also, it was common practice for males, and all the treaty signers were male, to assume several names throughout their lives. Translations wrought further confusion. For some treaties there were language chains linking one native dialect to another, then to French, and finally to English. The result, when eventually they were written down, was a perplexing, at times impenetrable, tangle. These Dakota names offer an example.

> Wahpekute (wahpe, leaf; kute, to shoot: "shooters in the leaves") One of the 7 primary divisions of the Dakota.[33]
> ...the man's titular name was Wacouta, "The Shooter," a title traditionally given the principal chief of his band, but I find... War de Cau ta, "who shoots in the pine tops"...The band was also known—in William Clark's words—as "the Sioux who shoot in the Pine Tops."[34]

Unsurprisingly the name is found with yet another variation on a Portage des Sioux peace treaty, Warseconta, "shoots in the Pine tops."

The signers at Portage des Sioux were not necessarily prominent tribal leaders. Of some three hundred natives listed on the treaties I found perhaps forty mentioned in other sources. Clark, Zebulon Pike, and other frontier explorers frequently recorded observations or conversations with natives in their journals. Working with the explorers' accounts and a register of treaty names I began to see whom the U.S. was dealing with when it named its tribes and made peace at Portage des Sioux.

Minnesota's Dakota, listed as Sioux on the treaties, must have presented a problem for the commissioners. At least six Dakota who signed one treaty in 1815 signed another one a year later. In the first year, Tantangamania—"the Walking Buffalo," Haisanwee—"the Horn," and Ampahaa—"the Speaker," signed on behalf of a tribe known as "the Sioux of the Lakes." In the ensuing year they must have found new affiliation. By that second year they were representing "eight bands of the Sioux, comprising the three tribes called the Sioux of the Leaf, the Sioux of the Broad Leaf, and the Sioux who shoot in the Pine tops." Three other men, Enigmanee—"that Flies as he Walks," Wasoukapaha—"the Falling Hail," and Manpinsaba—"the Black Cloud," represented the Sioux of the River St. Peter in 1815. By 1816 they, too, were Sioux of the Leaf, Broad Leaf, or shooters in the Pine tops.

The Dakota weren't the only ones representing multiple tribes. Sunawchewome and Mucketepoke represented the Pottawatomi one year and the Ottawa and Chippewa the next. Of course their names were spelled differently each time they were written. Evidently the business of naming tribes and making peace was inexact, an evolution favoring agreement and consolidation.

To return, the stated purpose of the Portage des Sioux treaties was peace. The Yankton, Osage, Omaha, Poncara, Kansa, Ottoes, Pawnee, Iowa and Winnebagoes represented about half the signatory tribes in the treaties of Portage des Sioux. Each of these tribes has a specific rite associated with making peace. Each tribe also has a gens whose function is to preserve and administer the peace rites. The Osage tribe offers a particularly good example of how peace is incorporated within tribal organization. Half of the Osage gens are dedicated to peace. The Tsizhe Washtage gens, the Dawn People, are keepers of the Osage peace rite.

> ...if a warrior of a hostile tribe steals into camp intent on doing harm and is detected and pursued, should he by chance flee into the house of one of these people he is saved. The red dawn that promises a clear and calm day is emblematic of peace to this gens. For ceremonial purposes this red dawn was symbolized by a feather taken from the undertail covert of an eagle and dyed red.[35]

The Winnebago have a similar organization and tradition.

> The lodge of the...(Thunderbird clan) is the peace lodge, over which the chief of the tribe presides, and in which disputes...are adjudicated...an offender or prisoner escaping to it was protected as long as he was within its precincts.[36]

The native concept of formally organizing peace and refuge was widespread in America. Some southern tribes made refuge available on a very broad scale.

> Towns of refuge existed among the Cherokee, the Creek, and probably other tribes...Echota, the ancient Cherokee capitol near the mouth of the Little Tennessee, was the Cherokee town of refuge, commonly designated as the "white town," or "peace town."...Among the Creeks the town of...Coosa, on the Coosa river in Alabama was a town of refuge.[37]

There is no evidence that Portage des Sioux was such a peace town at the time of the council, or before. But many of the tribes summoned there were especially competent in practicing peace. In some cases tribal authority was vested according to competence in peaceful relations. Some of the attending tribes held peace rites annually, both amongst themselves and with other tribes. That tradition helps explain how tribes could travel to the council grounds and coexist there in the presence of enemies. The Ottoes and Missouris, for example, were at war with the Pawnee, Omaha and Kansa. Yet these tribes attended the council. To be sure, Clark took practical security measures. A stockade, gunboats, militia and native allies were all organized and deployed for maximum effect. For those respecting force, Clark provided an impressive display. But less obvious factors were also at work.

Across the river from Portage des Sioux, just down from the Palisades, was an ancient native pictogram, the Piasa bird. Set in a natural amphitheater above the river, it was thought to represent a Thunderbird, the native guardian of passage to the south. Père Marquette, the earliest French explorer of the Mississippi, described it as two beasts, though later observers only mention one. Painted in red, black and green, Marquette saw,

> ...Two monsters which at first made us afraid, and upon which the boldest savages dare not long rest their eyes. They are as large as a calf; they have horns on their heads like a deer, a horrible look, red eyes, a beard like a tiger's, a face somewhat like a man's, a body crowned with scales, and so long a tail that it winds all round the body passing above the head and going back between the legs, ending in a fish's tail.[38]

The Piasa of Marquette's day has since been reduced to rubble and drowned. Railroads blasted its amphitheater and the Corps of Engineers flooded what remained in creating Lake Alton during the 1930s. I'd read somewhere that a billboard replica of the Piasa had been erected on the river road. Watching for it from the channel, I paddled south from Portage des Sioux along the Illinois shore hoping to get a glimpse. Rocked by wakes from weekend speedboats I passed strings of barges fleeted up along the bank. Some roustabouts waiting for a tow looked down at me from the lip of a covered grain barge. They seemed bemused at my puny canoe. I asked directions from them, and later from picnickers on the island beaches. Everyone knew of the Piasa, but no one knew where it was.

At the outskirts of Alton, sure that I'd gone too far, I headed the canoe toward a grain elevator at the river's edge. As I landed a young man on the bank leaned over and netted a catfish. He told me where to find the Piasa and agreed to watch my canoe in the meantime. I tied off to one of the elevator stanchions while we small-talked local interests. He kept at his fishing, handling his pole with practiced nonchalance. I unloaded my bicycle. Before I'd finished he was netting another catfish. He said grain from the elevator was the key to his luck, free chum. Something about him was so familiar I took his picture. Looking back at it now I realize how much he resembles my brother.

Piasa, in the Illinois language, translates roughly as "man-devouring bird." The "legend" published at the present site is an admittedly modern fiction, as is the billboard rendition of the bird. The billboard bears little resemblance to Marquette's drawing, or a drawing done by an early Mississippi artist, Henry Lewis. The modern version looks far more like a griffin than a Thunderbird. A granite monument chiseled in the shape of an arrowhead tells tourists that chief Ouatoga offered his life at the site in sacrifice to the man-eating Piasa. Just at the moment he was about to be clutched away, twenty of Ouatoga's followers simultaneously shot the giant monster dead. The chief, of course, was unharmed. By one account natives never failed to release arrows at the painted Piasa as they paddled past. Looking at the present day Piasa one could hardly blame them.

> Go yonder wherever the Missouri joins the Mississippi...at that place we...will be blessed...there will be a manitou who will give us everything...at that place, anyone at all could get something. That has been told to me. And at that place alone is where I can see a light.[39]
>
> The "red road" is that which runs north and south and is the good or straight way, for to the Sioux the north is purity and the south is the source of life.[40]

If the modern billboard Piasa has lost its power as a symbol, it nevertheless marks a place that once was potent in the eyes of natives. Clark, in choosing Portage des Sioux as the site for the peace council, was undoubtedly concerned first with accessibility. The village was convenient to the major rivers used by Midwestern natives. It was also close enough to St. Louis that he could obtain the force and provisions he needed in his role as council host. Just as important, the grounds were inconvenient enough that undue contact with St. Louis residents could be avoided. Some of those residents had little use for natives. The *Missouri Gazette* of 1815 openly vilified them. During council proceedings the *Gazette* ran a five-part series on native susceptibility to alcohol, promiscuity, native affinity for war and violence and other, similar topics. But Clark may have had other criteria in selecting Portage des Sioux. He had seen the Piasa bird and knew the importance of tradition to natives. Perhaps the winged pictogram, or the generous manitou, or the "red road" also figured in Clark's council grounds considerations.

Since learning of Portage des Sioux's council I have searched for the invitation Clark addressed to the thirty-seven tribes. Often mentioned in council correspondence, the invitation itself is lost. In its stead I offer the next few quotes. They sketch a composite invitation and hint at the proper protocol for invitation delivery.

> ...(natives) left a pouch of tobacco, an ear of corn, and a bearskin with a ring drawn around it on the ground, all of which signified their desire to smoke the same pipe, eat the same bread and sleep under the same roof.[41]

More likely than roof, the ring drawn on the ground probably symbolized an invitation to share the same sky. A Kansa representative to the Portage des Sioux council, Herocheshe, treated for peace years later with a village of Ottoes, Missouris and Iowas. His peace invitation to them also relied on images of smoking and eating.

> I have visited your village, that we might all smoke from the same pipe, and eat from the same bowl, with the same spoon, in token of our future union in friendship.

In that instance Herocheshe went on to explain his state of mind.

> On approaching your village, my friends and relatives, I thought I had not long to live. I expected that you would kill me, and these poor men who have followed me. But I received encouragement from the reflection, that if it should be my fate to die to-day, I would not have to die to-morrow, and I relied firmly upon the Master of Life.

One of Herocheshe's hosts answered him with equal candor.

> You observed that you were apprehensive of being killed as you approached our village, and you most probably would have been so, coming as you did, late in the evening, and without

the usual formality of sending a messenger to apprise us of your approach.[42]

Evidently, sometimes even messengers needed messengers. That certainly was the case with Clark's initial invitation to Black Hawk. One of his message bearers was killed. Without doubt, delivering peace invitations is dangerous work. Herocheshe allayed that danger with a kind of rational fatalism. He accepted that his mission might lead to death. Accepting death enabled Herocheshe to address enemies as friends and relatives, to offer them his pipe and his tobacco. Tobacco and the pipe are central to many aspects of native life, certainly to their tradition of peace. For natives, tobacco and its use are sacred. In Winnebago tradition tobacco was a gift of grandmother Earth, given first, before the gift of corn. Tobacco represents the primary condition of life. An invitation to smoke then, when extended to an enemy, was an invitation to establish with them the primary condition of life, peace.

> The first peace, which is the most important, is that which comes within the souls of men when they realize their relationship, their oneness, with the universe and all its Powers, and when they realize that at the center of the universe dwells Wakan-Tanka, and that this center is really everywhere, it is within each of us. This is the real Peace, and others are but a reflection of this. The second peace is that which is made between two individuals, and the third is that which is made between two nations. But above all you should understand that there can never be peace between nations until there is first that true peace which, as I have often said, is within the souls of men.[43]

The evening of my arrival at Portage des Sioux I camped on Portage Island. A steady stream of white egrets and blue herons flew past, low and silent, on their way to roost. Cicadas chirping in the trees were gradually replaced in song by peepers, an invisible, night-voicing frog. I went for a swim. Afterwards, leaning over a panful of white rice and eating slowly, I watched the sun go down. As light fell and the river took on its evening colors, profound loneliness came over me. It extended beyond the houseboats moored nearby or the orange horizon. It went beyond the previous week's birthday conversation with my father and beyond the bad dream brought on by my house tenant. My loneliness extended beyond the source of the Mississippi to why I had begun my trip in the first place. I had hoped somewhere along the river's length to find the great American peace. I had no criteria for recognizing it, only knowledge that such a thing must exist. Sitting there on Portage Island, after having paddled halfway down the continent, though deeply centered and calm, I felt alone. Halfway downriver, by now I was halfway absorbed into this great artery of the continent. It was as though my heartbeats were being dispersed or diluted and were no longer entirely my own. The river was by now entirely familiar and even perhaps a friend. But it was too relentless to share sympathy or desire. It was not half human or half of me.

Not all native pipe ceremonies are associated with peace. Far from it. War pipes were common in the time of the council at Portage des Sioux. Many important tribal matters have an associated pipe ritual. More than anything else, sharing a pipe in native tradition means unity. The pipe itself symbolizes unity. Its bowl represents earth and the stuff people are made of. Its stem is the path of life, the "red road," and the windpipe of Wakan-Tanka. To share a pipe is to share His breath. Pipe ceremony acknowledges Wakan-Tanka's presence in all directions, including the earth and sky. Using the pipe unites one in the harmonious breath of life, places one on the earth's straight path. I'm sure that to natives at Portage des Sioux sharing the sacred pipe held greater significance than signing paper treaties.

> The cosmos surrounding the pipe is spherical...In communal smoking the ritual also indicates the cosmos of social relationships. At the center is the self, the one holding the pipe. Next comes the circles...of human relationships; family, clan, and "nation." Further outward is the sphere of animal relations: those who fly in the sky above, and those who crawl on the earth below or swim in the sea. Finally there is the sphere of the most powerful spirits: the Four Directions (Winds), the Sky and the Earth (Sea). Together these four spheres of being form "all my relations."[44]

A pipe used in native peace rituals often has certain traditional decorations. Eagle feathers are frequently attached to the pipe stem. They represent the eagles, or Thunderbirds, that led people from the sky to earth in four soaring circles.

> The sky mentioned...here...is not the material sky that surrounds us, but the sky of conduct of men toward one

another, a sky which might be overcast with dangerous and destructive clouds of war, but which could be influenced by men, through self-restraint, self-denial, and good will, which alone can avert the storms of hatred and malice, and make the sky of conduct clear and serene...the Honga, the sacred (Imperial or Spotted) eagle came from above, in four circles, alighting upon the earth, to make it his abode. In like manner you have come from above to make the earth your abode.[45]

Since Wanbli Galeshka (the spotted eagle) flies the highest of all created creatures and sees everything, he is regarded as Wakan-Tanka under certain aspects. He is a solar bird, His feathers being regarded as rays of the sun, and when one is carried or worn by the Indian it represents, or rather is, the "Real Presence."...the wearer actually becomes the eagle, which is to say that he identifies himself, his real Self, with Wakan-Tanka.

The Spotted Eagle corresponds exactly...(to) the Intellect... often expressed as being a ray emanating from...the spiritual sun. From this it should be clear what is really being expressed in the often misunderstood song: "Wanbli galeshka wana ni he o who e," "The Spotted Eagle is coming to carry me away."[46]

In many ceremonies the pipe is elevated before the people on forked sticks. The sticks are its resting-place, thought by some to represent elk horns. Similar horns were described on the head of the Piasa bird. Perhaps to be carried away by the Piasa, with its wings of the air, scales of the sea and horns of the earth, was not necessarily to be devoured.

Portage des Sioux's small public library was indefinitely closed when I visited. The librarian had been incapacitated for some time with migraines. I resolved to research the village and its council as soon as I arrived in St. Louis, thirty miles downstream. I called Gene, my publisher at *Limelight*, to tell him I'd be arriving the next day with plans to stay about a week. He had offered me accommodations and an assurance that the city had several excellent libraries. We agreed to meet in the afternoon at Laclede's Landing, on St. Louis' north waterfront. While making my goodbyes I learned that Portage des Sioux's fleet, mostly pleasure craft, would be blessed from the shrine on the next morning. Over five hundred vessels were expected. I could just about see them, like the thousands of canoes, all gathered at the waterfront.

In late July's slanting afternoon I prepared to leave Portage des Sioux. The unclouded sun, already turning red, tinged the bowed white mantle of the river's patroness. Water- skiers, barely clad, waved as they passed by. Pushing my canoe from the concrete pier it struck me that Mary had supplanted the Piasa. The river's manitou had been exchanged for a madonna.

> We have been told by the white men, or at least by those who are Christian, that God sent to men His son, who would restore order and peace upon the earth; and we have been told that Jesus the Christ was crucified, but that he shall come again at the Last Judgement, the end of this world or cycle. This I understand and know that it is true, but the white men should know that for the red people too, it was the will of Wakan-Tanka, the Great Spirit, that an animal turn itself into a two-legged person in order to bring the most holy pipe to His people; and we too were taught that this White Buffalo Cow Woman who brought our sacred pipe will appear again at the end of this "world," a coming which we Indians know is not very far off.[47]

The next morning's camp was so alive with mosquitoes that I skipped breakfast. After locking through the Alton dam I took the river's own channel toward St. Louis. I could have taken an alternate route. The Corps of Engineers maintains a seven mile man-made canal for navigation on the Illinois side. But I'd had my fill of jockeying with barges. The canal's traffic was bound to be worse than I wanted to contend with. So I made a dubious choice and paid for it later at the Chain of Rocks.

River charts don't mark the Chain and fishermen who'd warned me about it differed in their accounts regarding how dangerous it was. Some said the Chain of Rocks was no more than a ripple, while others talked of a fifteen foot waterfall. I approached the rocks with more trepidation than sense. Past experience in rapids on much smaller rivers had taught me that mid-channel often has the deepest water. On small rivers mid-channel is the best place to avoid trouble. But the Mississippi is no small river and finding deep water is hardly a problem. Unfortunately, I positioned myself in midstream. If I'd been able to see the ledge known as the Chain of Rocks I definitely would have paddled to shore and portaged.

The ledge falls off so steeply that it's invisible from upriver. Sitting in my canoe's low seat was like looking down from the topmost of two overlapping plates of glass. The falls form an imperceptible seam. I heard them first, and by then my options were few. The ledge, a dam really, leads from either shore in two segments that join downstream forming a V. Being in midstream I was headed toward the apex, carried forward by a steadily accelerating current. I considered back-paddling to skirt the falls, meanwhile floating steadily closer to the ledge, weighing my fate, wondering whether to run the gauntlet.

A pair of medieval-style towers flank the Chain of Rocks. They rise several stories from the river, abandoned and windowless. I could have reached the one closest to the Illinois side. Taking refuge there I could have clung to the smooth stones, prolonging my decision, or waiting for help. It would have done no good. I would still have been the river's prisoner. Instead I snapped pictures of the towers, zipped my life vest closed and stowed all my loose gear in the forward compartment. I took my glasses off and buttoned them into a pocket. Sitting cross-legged in the very bottom of the canoe, I wedged my knees tight within the gunwales. As the river's power rose to a pounding din I paddled steadily, trying to stifle fear and maintain control. In a climax of spray I crested the falls. Suddenly my canoe was falling, pointed into a backwashed wall of boiling foam. Sun-brilliant water rose and fell all around me, roaring as though I had transgressed the boundaries of this world. The spray caused a beautiful rainbow to form arcing up from the river's boil. Caught in the maelstrom it was as though I were entering the earth itself. I couldn't see, or feel, or hear anything but the presence and power of the river. Then, just as suddenly I was spit out beyond the Chain of Rocks. Turbulence from the cascade swirled me round to face where I had been, congratulating my survival like a friend. Almost leisurely I bailed water from my swamped canoe, pouring it slowly, watching it fall sparkling and harmless into the river.

My luck was short-lived. Brazen by success I approached the next wing dam as stupidly as I had the Chain of Rocks. This time the current swept my canoe sideways and a rock punctured it just above the water line. I had grown careless, fatigued by days of endless paddling and heat. I limped into Laclede's Landing like a muddy piece of flotsam washed up on the cobblestones. A street person staggered past, tripping over cable moorings. He was muttering loudly, but his words were too garbled to understand. Though it was a very hot afternoon he wore a frayed knit cap and a heavy, long-sleeved shirt. He let himself to the ground as I pulled my canoe from the water. I bent to lock the canoe's crossbrace to a mooring cable, securing it so that I could leave and call Gene. When I finished and turned around, the man was facing me, sitting perhaps fifty yards away. He smiled broadly and waved as though he'd been expecting my arrival.

My first days in St. Louis were relaxed. I took time to repair my canoe, to sleep in the afternoon and to read. Gene was a wonderful host. But each day he grew more concerned and agitated. His wife was very ill and getting worse. Her condition became acute, diagnosed finally as a herniated ulcer. My visit was an unneeded burden for their troubled household, so I took a room in a vacant dormitory at Washington University. By bus, and sometimes on my bicycle, I visited libraries and researched river history. At the Mercantile Library I studied beneath Catlin's paintings. At Central Library I found microfilm of the *Missouri Gazette* in the time of the council at Portage des Sioux. At the Missouri Historical Society I learned of Cahokia, the largest native civilization of ancient North America. Cahokia intrigued me with its giant mounds only a few miles away across the Mississippi. All of these were reason enough to stay for a while in St. Louis. But another, special, and more personal purpose detained me. The third night of my visit Gene had introduced me to Margaret Wallace. By the time I arrived he knew I was a bachelor and he asked if I'd like a date. Two months alone on the river was plenty for me.

"Do you want to meet a fast girl, or a nice girl?"

"A nice one."

Gene coached me through a phone conversation, my speech coming slowly as a winter thaw.

"Tell her your name. Tell her you're a friend of Gene Liss and you're a stranger in town. Tell her you'd like to get a cup of coffee, would she have time to take you."

Margaret was the reason that I stayed.

Our first evening together Margaret took me for coffee at an outdoor Italian cafe. We sat at a small table, close to one another beneath an ornate gaslight from the turn of the century. Her dark auburn hair, unfastened and natural, curled away free, catching the street light in a red-sheened halo. I was entranced by her guileless face, so young and fair. Her eyes, like her hair, were dark, too. But in them the fire was centered, controlled and glowing as though instilled with calm. An antique porcelain cameo fastened the collar of her linen blouse. She was composed in features fine, clear and timeless. They were delicate as a lingering glance, or a finger trailed in the water. We talked in low, quiet tones, my bass and her alto, like flowers in a garden, like jazz notes in the nighttime. I tried to order a trendy ice drink, a frizzante. But the cafe's ice machine was broken. Next I selected gelato from the menu and found that it, too, was unavailable. In the end I settled on scotch and was happier for the inconvenience. So was Margaret.

Her grandmother had told her once that men who drank scotch could generally be trusted, a trait learned perhaps during Prohibition.

We talked of journeys. Around us, from the other simple chairs and small tables, hundreds of other voices drifted upwards, lazily found a stratum and became the hum of a summer night. My own words came slowly, as though I'd forgotten how to speak. I picked an impatiens from a nearby planter and offered it to her. She drew me out of myself until it seemed that I'd told my whole life. Then she said it was time to leave. Driving back in her white convertible, night air slipped over the windshield becoming turbulent at our passing. Watching then as she drove away, matching her simple wave, I knew that Margaret had moved through me as well.

Two days later we met again. We went to lunch with a friend of hers and then, after work, had iced coffees together. We bought a picnic of salmon, raspberries, bread, cheese, wine and chocolate to eat in Forest Park, on the grounds of 1904's World Fair. Around us people were walking to games on the ball fields. The national anthem began to play from a radio somewhere in the stands behind the nearest diamond. I spread the picnic and realized we didn't have a corkscrew. Margaret tore a heel from our loaf of bread and began to eat. "I've never done that before," she said. I fumbled with the wine bottle, trying to use keys as a corkscrew. It was futile. Finally I just pushed the cork in. By then she had torn another piece of bread and was offering it to me. I filled our paper cups and tried to toast with a poem I'd copied from her book of Yeats. But I couldn't remember it well enough and in the end had to read from the scrap I carried in my shirt pocket.

> "*Wine comes in at the mouth*
> *And love comes in at the eye;*
> *that's all we know for truth*
> *Before we grow old and die.*
> *I lift this glass to my mouth,*
> *I look at you, and I sigh.*"[48]

We had not enough time. Margaret was to meet her cousin and his wife before they returned to Spain. He is an engineer for McDonnell Douglas, assigned to troubleshoot F-18 Eagles in the Spanish Air Force. She took me along to a tavern, a trendy sports bar papered with photos of Cardinal baseball heroes. Drinking whiskey, her cousin said better things of the F-18s than of their Spanish pilots. Charley, Margaret's brother, came by a little later. He told how a pilot friend of his had died in the Gulf War. Margaret's cousin guessed that Charley's friend had been flying an A-6 and how it had been shot down. He said the plane was a death trap unfit to fight a war in. Margaret, opposite me, was silent. Beside her, Charley, too, was quiet, absorbed I think with thoughts of his friend. I noticed then how much brother and sister resembled one another. And I noticed that Charley, though ten years my junior, looked an awful lot like me.

On the weekend Margaret and I traveled to Memphis for an exhibition on Catherine the Great. Margaret had been invited to stay at a country club, the guest of friends in the city. I took a room in another dormitory, Memphis State. We went twice to the exhibition because the show was related to Margaret's work. We went once down to Beale Street because both of us like the Blues. Sunday we returned to St. Louis. Monday I made bannock cakes in Margaret's kitchen, provisions for my continued journey.

In the afternoon of the last day of July, with summer's heat at its cusp, I went back to the river. The cabbie who took me there ventured that people envied me the silence out on the water. I was watching my canoe, tied none too securely atop his compact station wagon. We passed a bank's billboard thermometer. With two more degrees it would be reading triple digits. "Very early each morning," the cabbie said, "I rise and listen for everything to stop—the street traffic, the refrigerator, and all the other appliances in my apartment. It's quiet then, before the day." On reflex, and in the same wistful tone as his I replied, "It's cool in the morning." The cabbie helped unload my gear at the riverfront and I had him photograph me beside my canoe. I wanted to remember the silence he cherished, and the heat.

The landing was a hive of tourists. Many of them had arrived that morning on the *Delta Queen*. She was cabled to the same moorings where only days before I had cabled my canoe. A shuttling helicopter hovered noisily above a nearby concession barge. It choppered downtown and back like a worker bee, lifting people for its bug-eyed view. Replica paddlewheelers blasted long-short-short-long horn greetings to the *Delta Queen*. These smaller boats, named for Mark Twain's characters, carry the short-haul tourists. Compared to the stately *Queen*, they were little more than nymphs. Overhead a blimp crawled across the sky. Like a fat drone it lumbered aimlessly, detached from the frenetic activity of the landing.

Silence. It was odd to be canoeing again. My arms were numb and the seat seemed unnaturally high. It was as though I were suspended above the river by surface tension alone, striding like a water spider. I felt strength in my paddle again, now that I was rested, and I pulled it against the current's solid swiftness. Skimming past the landing I thought of the cabbie. He was right to envy me, but not for any outward silence. Motile tranquility, the living silence within, was my treasure. Towboats passed, traffic resonated on an interstate bridge above, and from midchannel the *Becky Thatcher* laid on its horn. But I felt stillness. The silence of the river, moving and unending, was within me. No longer lonely, I re-entered the freedom of the river.

Hooped over the St. Louis landing, drawing energy from the earth it escapes and the sky it captures, is the river's most colossal witness. Its eyes look upon the mounds of Cahokia, and the Chain of Rocks and the city. It rises from the earth with massive effort, spending temptation toward the threshold of heaven, tapering to a focus: then it begins to remember, to acquire moments of history, to descend, massive once again, to the earth. It is an architectural parable of steel, telling time's message from beginning to end: creation and birth lead to life which leads to death and someday, to the apocalypse. The Gateway Arch is the river's paradigm. It parallels the river in form and symbol, compressing the river's flow and round earth span to a simple, stainless, human scale. It is the native's sacred hoop, gilded silver, stretched and upended.

Beneath the Arch, in the museum at its foundation, are Indian peace medals. Like seeds of tranquillity they are planted in the earth, centering the whole ellipse only half described by the skyborn Arch. Peace medals were very highly regarded by natives. Even Black Hawk wore his medals to the grave. American presidents began giving medals during Washington's term, continuing a European practice from the 1600's. The last American medals were handed out in 1896. Generally medals were oval in shape, cast in silver. A presidential likeness filled the obverse while the reverse side presented various symbols of friendship and goodwill. These tokens, the peace medals, are hard and lasting evidence of an exchange of peace.

"Among the articles to be sent out there will be some solid silver medals," wrote Secretary of War James Monroe to Governor Clark. The medals sent to Portage des Sioux most likely bore the image of President Madison. Several are on display at the Arch museum. They are inscribed with Madison's name, title and the date of his first inauguration, 1809. On the reverse are clasped hands, one extending from a buttoned sleeve representing the government, the other bare like a native's. Pictured above the clasped hands are two pipes, one conventional, the other a hatchet pipe. Hatchet pipes were a popular

Indian trade good of the day. Also on the reverse side is the inscription, "Peace and Friendship."

The pipes represented on the medals scarcely resemble those used in native peace rites, calumets. They are not decorated with eagle feathers nor rested on pipe-stands. The hatchet pipe especially, belies an authentic pipe of peace. At best it promotes some European notion of utility and at worst it associates peace with an instrument of war. Still, the medals were only meant as tokens. They are our tangible artifacts from the great council held at Portage des Sioux.

St. Louis has replaced Cahokia just as barges and speedboats have replaced canoes. The statue of Our Lady of the Rivers, with its neon halo, has replaced the horned image of the Piasa bird. Sleepy Portage des Sioux barely remembers the ancient village of Tamaroa natives. But the peace medals endure. They are effective reminders of America's history. Some, bright as the Arch itself, appear as though newly minted. Others, much warmer in appearance, are nearly smooth, worn from long carriage at some person's breast. Like the Arch, the medals speak eloquently of a transition in culture. Both reflect the circular unity within which right relationships are maintained. The Gateway Arch, shimmering in the passing sun, is an invitation, a circle drawn round, that all peoples might sleep together under one clear sky. Dormant in the ground beneath it are the medals, seeds of peace sown when America was still very young.

In sacred native rituals the peace pipe is not lit with an open flame. It is lit with embers, sometimes drawn from a fire extinguished by a covering of earth. The embers initiate sacred offerings by connecting the past to the present. From earth and the past comes light for peace— peace within, between and among human beings. The peace medals are embers too, seeds of light left by people of another age.

"At that place alone I can see a light," the sacred buffalo said of the area where the Missouri meets the Mississippi. "To our people this offering means that you wish peace, and that you wish to establish a relationship with us. Is it for this reason that you have brought such a sacred offering?"

"Yes!...we wish to have a relationship with you which is as close as the relationship which exists between your people and Wakan-Tanka."[49]

Someday peace will not be left to chance. It will not be only an interval that follows war, or precedes it, a single side of a tossed coin.

True peace is within the souls of men, it lays there like a mark beside a name, like an ember, like a medal worn smooth from the heartbeats within one's breast.

Camino Real

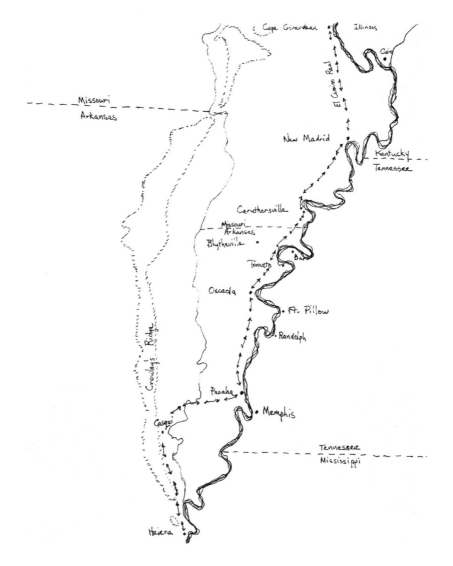

Cape Girardeau Illinois

Cairo

Missouri
Arkansas

El Camino Real

New Madrid

Kentucky
Tennessee

Caruthersville

Missouri
Arkansas

Blytheville

Tomato

Bar.

Osceola

Ft. Pillow

Randolph

Crowleys Ridge

Pacaha

Memphis

Casqui

Tennessee
Mississippi

Helena

Camino Real

Camino Real is Spanish for King's Highway. In St. Louis a street named Kingshighway leaves Calvary Cemetery, bisects the city North to South and then becomes Interstate 55 plunging down the continent toward Memphis. In the 1920's the Daughters of the American Revolution erected markers in the old river towns of Kimmswick, St. Genevieve, Cape Girardeau, New Madrid and Carruthersville to commemorate the frontier thoroughfare which first connected them, El Camino Real. But the king's highway was already old when the Spanish Crown first claimed rule in western America. The route was one of several in a network of trade connecting ancient civilizations in the Mississippi valley. Native traders had carried salt, copper and pipestone south into Arkansas for centuries before any Spaniard trod the route known as El Camino Real.

In 1953 Tennessee Williams wrote his dreamlike play, *Camino Real.* Williams was a native of St. Louis and the city commemorates his artistry with a brass star in the sidewalk along Delmar Boulevard. After he died he was buried in Calvary Cemetery, at the head of Kingshighway. Williams' play is particularly appropriate to the section of river south from St. Louis. In writing it Williams borrowed characters from the river's past, and foretold of others into its future. *Camino Real* opens with Don Quixote de la Mancha stumbling down the theatre's center aisle, a knight in rusted armor, fatigued, but still thirsting for adventure.

Yes, at daybreak tomorrow I will go on from here with a new companion and this old bit of blue ribbon to keep me in mind of the distance that I have gone and the distance I have yet to go...[50]

My first morning out of St. Louis I had coffee in Kimmswick, Missouri. Kimmswick has cashed in its red brick and clapboard charm for a piece of the tourist trade. At the town's only restaurant I waited with a bused-in crowd to be seated on plastic chairs. The river south of St. Louis has no charm left to cash. Rip-rap, dikes, levees, barge fleeting, loading and unloading terminals, tank farms, coal stockpiles and industrial plants line the banks. The river is contorted, restrained, pumped full of chemicals and regulated like a heart patient with bad arteries. South of St. Louis tows push barge strings three times larger than on the upper river. These forty-eight unit leviathans kick up seven foot waves, roiling the water behind them for a quarter mile. I met a kayaker who paddles in those wakes, claims they're the best whitewater in Missouri. But from St. Louis south river recreation on the Mississippi is an anomaly. For the most part the river is one big commercial project bought and paid for by the Army Corps of Engineers.

"What," I asked you, "is harmless about a dreamer, and what," I asked you, "is harmless about the love of the people?—Revolution only needs good dreamers who remember their dreams."[51]

Before leaving St. Louis I had arranged to picnic with Margaret in St. Genevieve on the coming Sunday. But by Friday morning I was already in that old French town. I bicycled through with the day so new that not even the bakery was open. Suspended wooden signs hung still in the morning light, lazily fronting the historic buildings as though they hadn't yet had their coffee. The signs told who built which building, and why, and when. I considered waiting in town for two days, nosing around the frontier interiors, museum displays and shops. But I telephoned Margaret instead. I woke her at a not-quite-civilized hour and we resituated our coming picnic to Cape Girardeau. Then I returned to the river. I had hoped to start paddling before the day's heat set in. At eight-thirty in the morning it was already eighty-five degrees.

That night coyotes cried as the sun went down. The river was very still, a perfect mirror of sympathy for the lonely howls. Echoes chased across the water, purifying the darkness, opening the gates of the night's black den. Summoned stars winked like fire eyes in the sky. Then a gentle wind stirred the river and tiny waves began to ferry reflections of the stars onto shore.

> *You really don't want to leave here. You think you don't want to go because you're brave as an old hawk. But the truth of the matter—the real truth not the royal truth—is that you're terrified of the Terra Incognita outside that wall.* [52]

Coming into Cape Girardeau the river turns sharply south past Devil's Island. The swiftest current on the whole river is on the outside of that bend. Towboats labor mightily to get past, cautious of the turn whether headed upstream or down. Cape's floodwall begins there, a long imposing plane of concrete. Doors worthy of Oz open from the levee onto the city's Main Street. But Cape Girardeau is no Oz. Cut off from any views of or commerce with the river the city is being slowly strangled into ruin. Shops and stores are boarded up and closed. In a nearby residential block eight of the ten homes had realty signs in their front yards.

I camped opposite town, on a sandbar, downstream from a highway bridge. While I was cooking my customary pan of rice somebody fired a rifle in my direction. Instinctively I dove flat onto the sand. Then another small caliber round rang out. The shots were coming from the levee's far side. I could hear the bullets hit rock, ricochet and cut the air above my head. Though the levee made an effective barricade, I was still alarmed. I hollered for the shooter to stop, but received no reply. Crawling toward the levee, I continued to shout as more rounds were fired. The bullets zipped overhead, whizzing out to die somewhere above the river. It was like being in a Western, except there was no music and the bullets were real.

When I reached the levee the gunfire ceased. I heard an ATV start up and sputter away. I waited, lying in the sand, looking back toward my tent and canoe, wondering if the shooter had gone, wondering if I should leave the sandbar. For the first time I noticed how much river trash littered the bar. A nearby stand of unsprouted willows held remnants of the spring flood: scraps of plastic bags, strands of synthetic tow rope, an old tire, a rusted barrel, white chunks of styrofoam, bottles and cans. Bits of refuse hung from the lifeless willow staffs like tattered pennants. The receding waters had pointed all of them downstream, dirtied them brown with mud and grass, speckled them green with bits of algae. Across the river a sandblaster worked monotonously taking paint off a barge. The gunfire did not resume. Uneasily, I stood and began walking back toward my camp. The campstove was no longer burning. Its pan of rice had boiled over and put out the flame.

The next morning Margaret arrived at our rendezvous, a church, precisely on time. As I looked up the street her white convertible crested the last hill between us. We stashed my bicycle in the church's garage and joined a stream of parishioners come to hear the service. Afterwards, she drove while I guessed at which turns to take until we found Trail of Tears State Park. I'd noticed the park and its boundaries on my river charts while coming into town. Its bluffs, several hundred feet high, command panoramic views of the Mississippi. It is an excellent place to picnic.

> *What else are we offered? The never-broken procession of little events that assure us that we and the strangers about us are still going on! Where? Why? And the perch that we hold is unstable! We're threatened with eviction, for this port of entry and departure, there are no permanent guests! And where else have we to go when we leave here?*[53]

On June 30, 1830 President Andrew Jackson signed the Indian Removal Act. The law removed Cherokee from Georgia and other eastern states west to Oklahoma. The last of the tribe were forced out under military escort in the winter of 1838-9. Of over eighteen thousand deportees, a quarter died along the way. Their path became known as the Trail of Tears. One branch of the trail crossed the Mississippi at the site of the park. Ferried over in midwinter, some of the natives were met by merciful residents offering food and clothing. But for others there was only death. Princess Otahki, for one, is buried in the park.

Margaret and I idled away the afternoon picnicking on a bluff above the river. She'd brought roast chicken, corn salad, banana bread, a split of wine, raspberry tarts, chocolates and more. Her picnicware was as pretty as the food was delicious: green Depression-glass plates and glasses, checkered cloth napkins, silverware and a cloth spread. We were totally free there then, enjoying each other, the day and the view of the river. We ended our meal as we had begun it, with a kiss that lasted like a prayer.

When we returned to town, my bike had been stolen from the church garage. I called the police and was told to wait for a reporting officer. Forty-five minutes later with evening coming on, Margaret took me back to the river. The police had not yet come and Margaret wanted a ride in my canoe. The canoe was cabled and locked, with my only lock, to a tree at the river, several hundred yards downstream of a highway bridge. In the morning when I had crossed the river coming into town I landed the canoe, cabled it and then climbed straight up the bank carrying my bike. The riverbank was steep, full of thorny underbrush, nettles and cockleburs. It was no place to take a lady.

To avoid the bracken we parked Margaret's car near the highway bridge and began picking a new way down the bank toward the river. A worn footpath led from the road's edge across some railroad tracks, along the bridge and then down. I grasped Margaret's hand and took the lead. As we ducked under the bridge girders our eyes slowly adjusted to the dimmer light. We saw a warren of broken lawn chairs, torn mattresses and flattened cardboard boxes. Someone, perhaps several people had jungled up there. Ashes of campfires and piles of empty cans ripened in the stale air. Undercutting their odor was the faint, sharp smell of latrine. Overhead traffic rumbled the bridge's length like a migraine. Margaret and I stepped gingerly through the maze, crunching broken glass underfoot. I became tenser with each step, concerned that she should be exposed to the obvious danger. As we descended through the limestone ledges that formed the bridge abutment I could hear men's voices coming up from the river.

Barge cables and giant chains lay strewn through the ledges and sand from flood level down to the water line. The broken fragments of frayed steel hawser trailed in twists and links from rock-set pitons. Like giant rusted snakes come out to sun they seemed to threaten our every step. Downstream further the ledges and rock deteriorated to a sandy beach. At the river's edge the sand gave way to mud. Well down the beach, perhaps twice the distance to my canoe, a group of men were talking. They looked older than we two. On sighting us one whistled a catcall and another pulled at the crotch of his pants. Most of them, five in all, were fishing. Their rods were set in forked sticks on the bank, lines heavily weighted out toward the channel. One, a loudmouth, was last to notice us. He reacted to the others' gaze, swinging 'round on his heel and then fixing us finally in an approximate, stuporous glare. Almost immediately he came stumbling toward us, holding out a milk jug as he came.

The man could have been any age, say fifty, was disheveled and unshaven. He came down the beach lurching and swaying, though his pace was steady enough. By then we were at my canoe. I whispered to Margaret to stay behind it and back-a-ways. The man was almost upon us as I dialed the cable's combination right, left and right again. My mind was spinning, too, trying to decide how to react, what to do.

Finally I had the cable loose and the canoe's forward compartment open. The man was very close by then. On reflex I grabbed for the paddle stowed in the bottom. I could already smell his breath pronouncing him in warm, sickly-sweet waves of alcohol. Turning up to face him I felt nauseous. I lifted the paddle up abruptly, almost violently holding it out before me. Facing him then I could see his stagnant pupils, pale as a blind man's. I frightened him. My face and ears were hot with adrenaline. I towered over the frail man and realized in the same instant that I frightened myself as well.

Clouds of alcohol reeked from his person and rose like a genie from the jug he carried. The liquid, much too red for wine, must have been Kool-Aid with a spike. He asked if we wanted a drink. "No!" I said too loudly, and started dragging the canoe toward the river. He righted himself, a rambling loudmouth once more, and offered to push us off. Margaret took the canoe's only seat. I sat on the canoe's floor and faced her. The man talked the whole while, questioning really, and then finally pushed us from the muddy bank into the river. I looked down at my paddle's blade then, harmless in the water. I despised the club it might have been. Looking up at Margaret I wondered if this was how she imagined my canoeing life to be.

We rode the current out to the main channel. Turning toward the far shore we saw a deer walk out of the willows for a drink. He was a buck with a medium-sized rack totally unconcerned by our presence. Drivers on the bridge above us honked their car horns and waved. At dusk we returned to shore. I helped Margaret put the top up on her convertible for the drive back to St. Louis. She gave me a couple bags of homemade cookies, Snickerdoodles, for my journey. I'd told her they were my favorite kind. I went back to the river. By then the men had built a fire and were gathered around it, talking as before. Silently I launched my canoe alone and crossed to my camp on the opposite shore.

> *Yes, the most dangerous word in any human tongue is the word for brother. It's inflammatory.—I don't suppose it can be struck out of the language altogether but it must be reserved for strictly private usage in back of soundproof walls. Otherwise it disturbs the population...*[54]

The next day's early afternoon found me walking into Cairo, Illinois for my mail. Unfortunately I was too late. The Post Office had held the mail for ten days and then sent it back. General delivery is supposed to be held for thirty. Like the bike, here was my second spate of bad news and though I'm not superstitious I know how luck runs. Feeling somewhat burdened I sought out Cairo's library and found it to be a beautiful old building. It has a water fountain from the turn of the century in its vestibule. The fountain is cast all of a piece with fruited vines, painted, climbing the front and sides. A wave motif along the top evokes water images of clouds and river. Steps for children flank either side so they can help themselves over the basin. The fountain wets them in their thirst for knowledge.

Walking back to the river I found Cairo's memorial to the Gulf War. It must have been one of the first permanent Gulf memorials in the country. In other river towns I had seen billboards with local serviceman and women listed by name, rank and service branch, American flags, big yellow ribbons and the slogan, "Support Our Troops in Operation Desert Storm." But Cairo's memorial was done in granite. In a wedge-shaped park a little brick walkway ran a short distance to a flagpole. The walk was flanked with shrubs and by markers naming the soldiers. Below the pole at the walk's end was a headstone inscribed with Cairo's Guard unit. At the headstone's top was an engraved sunburst lettered, "Desert Storm."

I once had a pony named Peeto. He caught in his nostrils the scent of thunderstoms coming even before the clouds had crossed the Sierra...[55]

The Ohio joins the Mississippi just below Cairo and swells the river to over a mile wide. For days I couldn't get used to the river's new size. It made me feel both bigger and smaller at the same time. Bigger because one couldn't help but participate in the river's new immensity and power. And yet one couldn't help but feel very small as well. The bigger river was completely open, unshaded and impersonal as a mall parking lot. And it was hot. All the way from Minnesota the river and the weather had grown progressively warmer. But below Cairo the weather got just plain hot. Shriveling hot. There wasn't any shade on the river anymore.

Approaching a loop of river that winds into New Madrid, Missouri at eight o'clock in the morning, it was ninety-five degrees. I wondered if I could portage that New Madrid bend. My charts showed two miles of land bridging thirty miles of river. I drifted on the current, pondering. Some commercial fishermen were pulling nets from a shallow bay into their flatbottom. I could see their pickup and trailer parked at a landing on the levee ahead. The sky was cloudless and the day's heat promised to be brutal. I paddled over to the fisherman with no more than a "howdy" and asked which way they were headed. We talked back and forth and I offered to trade a bag of cookies for a ride across the New Madrid oxbow. The boat's driver laughed, but I told him he didn't know yet how good the cookies were. An hour later I was across the oxbow with a bag of ice to boot.

I reached Carruthersville, Missouri that night, done in with heat stroke. From a pay telephone I tried Margaret, hoping that she'd not yet left for her vacation in northern Michigan. Her recorded message told me I was too late. I was feverish, exhausted and crushed with disappointment. I wanted to be someplace cool. I wanted to give up my foolish journey. For the allotted three minutes I poured a tale of weariness and woe into the receiver. It would shame me if I heard it today. Walking back towards the river I was offered a ride by a man and his son in their restored '51 Mercury. The pair had been cruising the riverfront, had seen my canoe and decided to go looking for the canoeist. Since Carruthersville isn't very big they didn't have much trouble spotting me. I was beginning to look like the vagrant I had become. My new friends toured me past the city's highlights, the new Wal-Mart and the City Park. I took a picture of them at the park, in front of their pale green car. A building's red brick wall and faded letters of a Coca-Cola advertisement formed the backdrop. In the foreground beside them was a granite boulder, the southernmost monument marking El Camino Real.

> *Do you feel yourself spiritually unprepared for the age of exploding atoms? Do you distrust the newspapers? Have you arrived at a point on the Camino Real where the walls converge not in the distance, but right in front of your nose?*[56]

The next day, August 8th, I met a farmer on the Tennessee bank who'd come down to the river to watch the west for rain. Leamond Arthur had picked watermelons all day on his farm and had chosen one out of the thousands to eat. He'd ridden his ATV over a half-mile wide sand dune separating his farm from the river intending to sit on the bank and enjoy his fruit. But after cutting the melon in half he'd found that it was sour. When I paddled up he was looking out pensively over the river. He sat astride his ATV, arms crossed and resting on the handlebars. In another age he would have been sitting astride a horse and leaning over the saddle's pommel. He wore a light plaid, pearl-buttoned shirt and jeans with a wide leather belt wound in trim at the edges. The beltbuckle was a small shield. His Levis were faded and his Western boots were prowed like the bow of my canoe. At fifty Leamond is the youngest person in Bar Community, Tennessee because all of the younger people have gone. His wife is gone, too, drawn away by a world larger than a few homes and a big farm.

Leamond said he'd listened to the commodities report on the radio for the few days previous, learning projected prices for his crops. Soybeans had fallen the limit on the Chicago Exchange for two days running. Rain in the North had increased the nation's crop projections and ruined the soybean market. The day I met him he hadn't had the stomach to listen. Instead, he'd come down to the river to watch for rain, and perhaps an end to his farm's drought.

Overhead a pair of B-52's circled lazily as we talked. Leamond said they were nuclear S.A.C. bombers headed into Eaker Air Force Base at Blythville, Arkansas. All of the years since Viet Nam those planes had been the very embodiment of war for me. But I had never seen one fly. Watching them then I felt nothing but coldness. Leamond said that Eaker was scheduled to close. I wondered out loud what new work the people there would do.

As we parted, he on his ATV and I in my canoe, I noticed his opened watermelon. It was lying where he had dropped it, atop a dune of sand at the water's edge, red flesh speckled with seeds. Its insides looked much like a human's while its outside looked like a bomb. I thought to myself, "How strange." I thought of my farming background, how we used to wait and pray for rain, how we used to eat watermelons right out of the field. I thought about the bombers. August is the anniversary of Hiroshima and Nagasaki. In La Crosse people would be putting peace lanterns on the river to commemorate victims of the atomic blasts. Years ago Yoko Ono had sent a peace lantern to La Crosse. On it was a simple line drawing of two people embracing. I paddled away from the sand bar watching the sky, hoping for Leamond Arthur's sake it would rain.

Eaker, the base Leamond said was closing, was considered for siting rail-based Peacekeeper nuclear missiles in 1988. During site evaluations remains of at least ten ancient natives were unearthed. A new law, the Native Americans Graves Protection and Repatriation Act of November 1990, required that the native remains be re-interred. In 1991, the year of my journey, Robert Whitebird performed the reburial ceremony. At age seventy-eight he is the last full-blooded male Quapaw. The Quapaw tribe occupied northeast Arkansas at the time of European colonization. They are thought to have descended from the civilizations that greeted

Hernando DeSoto when he arrived at the Mississippi—the Aquixo, Casqui, Pacaha and Quigate. Eaker's public affairs officer witnessed the Quapaw reburial and asked Mr. Whitebird what significance tobacco played in the ceremony. Mr. Whitebird shrugged, chuckled and replied, "It's always been done that way."

Generalissimo, the Survivor is no longer surviving. I think we'd better have some public diversion right away. Put the Gypsy on! Have her announce the Fiesta![57]

The next morning I bailed an inch and a half of rain from my canoe and then paddled into Osceola, Arkansas. Osceola's public library was decked out to celebrate Elvis International Memorial week, scheduled to coincide with the anniversary of "The Death." No one in these parts need ask whose death "The Death" refers to. Elvis pins and buttons, magazine clippings and a patchwork quilt depicting Elvis hits were on display. A guitar was propped up behind the counter and books idolizing the rock 'n' roller were set on edge atop the shelves. The librarian, a woman in perhaps her mid-forties, epitomized style fashions of Presley's heyday. She wore cat-eye rhinestoned glasses. Her hair was a bouffant worn long and flipped just above her shoulders. She had a full, pleated, white and print dress belted at the waist. It buttoned over her bodice to open at a starched Peter Pan collar. She, another man and I were the only people in the library. I saw her furtively steal more than one languorous glance over the stacks toward the other man. At closing time she gave me the bum's rush, but not so the other man. When I left she locked the doors behind me.

Osceola was named for a Seminole chief of the 1830's who was warred against by President Jackson. Osceola suffered the all-too-common indignities of being a native chief in the way of progress: betrayal, forced removal and manipulation. Worse, his wife was sold into slavery by the local Indian Agent. One time Osceola stabbed a treaty paper with his knife rather than sign it. "The land is ours, that is the way I sign," he said. This and other acts caused the government to clap Osceola in irons. Imprisoned in Fort Moultrie, South Carolina in 1838 he became dejected, refused to eat and died. Ennobled in martyrdom, Osceola became a popular public name and so replaced the previous name for Plum Point, Arkansas.

He stood as a planet among the moons of their longing, haughty with youth, a champion of the prize-ring![58]

94

I sat for a haircut in Osceola hoping to improve my appearance and so to look a little less the vagrant. For small talk I asked the barber what he knew of river history. He told me that during the Civil War a regiment of blacks had been driven into the river and drowned at a bluff south of town. The bluff, the first of four Chickasaw bluffs, was known then as Fort Pillow. The fort was established by Confederates and overlooked the river forty-five miles above Memphis. The Confederates abandoned Fort Pillow in 1862 and Union forces, half of whom were former slaves, garrisoned the post. Confederate General Nathan Bedford Forrest, a slave trader prior to the war, attacked Fort Pillow on April 12th, 1864. The Fort's main defensive feature was a single earthen embankment. The Confederates stormed it and literally drove the Union forces into the river. Of the 262 blacks stationed at Fort Pillow, 204 were killed. A Confederate soldier wrote afterwards, "The poor deluded Negroes would run up to our men, fall on their knees with uplifted hands and scream for mercy, but were ordered to their feet and then shot down." An investigation was called, but eventually enthusiasm for it waned. General Forrest, unrepentant, had this to say: "The river was dyed red with the blood of the slaughtered for 200 yards. It is hoped that these facts will demonstrate to the northern people that Negro soldiers cannot cope with Southerners."[59]

General Forrest is still a hero to some Southerners. Public monuments in Memphis extol his virtues. "Fame's hoofbeats die not...the greatest commander of light cavalry" says the plaque beneath a bronze life-sized statue of the mounted general. Some days later, in Vicksburg, Mississippi there was more. Gordon Cotton is curator of the Vicksburg City Museum, housed in the town's ante-bellum courthouse. He has donated his great-grandfather's Ku Klux Klan hood for display, a relic of his great-grandfather's participation in the Klan during the Reconstruction era. His ancestor, William Price Cotton, had been a private in the CSA. Here is how Gordon Cotton recounts the history of his ancestor's Klan:

> Confederate veterans organized the Ku Klux Klan in Pulaski, Tennessee in 1866. The Klan spread rapidly throughout the South. Gen. Nathan B. Forrest was elected to head the group which at its peak numbered about 500 thousand men. Gen. Forrest disbanded the Klan in 1869 though some chapters continued to operate independently until 1876. Its purpose was to rid the South of Carpetbag-Scalawag-Black governments, which were often corrupt. Secrecy was necessary to protect the members from reprisals by federal troops, but because of

secrecy, atrocities were sometimes attributed to the Klan by unscrupulous individuals. Many people suffered, some no doubt innocently, as the Klan tried to restore some semblance of decency to the government. The original Klan was in no way connected, other than by name, to later and present-day organizations.

Gordon's office is in the old bailiff's room at the foot of the stairs. You have to go past his office to get to the Klan exhibit upstairs. More accessible is another of Gordon's exhibits just inside the entrance. It is titled "Lift Dat Bale" and accompanies a photo of a dock laborer named John Louse.

> The Negro roustabouts who loaded the bales of cotton and other products aboard the steamboats have become legendary because of their strength and their songs. They found time to express their feelings, both happiness and sorrow, in melody and dancing, strumming the banjo, shuffling their feet as they "Jumped Jim Crow," improvising rhythms to the bouncing of the gangplank, giving birth to the "Coonjine," a happy chant which helped eased their burdens…

I talked with Gordon outside the museum, on the perimeter of its grounds. He'd just finished spraying an old live oak for termites and was taking a break. I stood on the sidewalk several steps below him in the tree's shade. Grey beards of Spanish moss hung from the tree branches like eavesdropping spectators. Gordon and I discussed trees and moss, insecticides, resistance, natural adaptation and the outcome of generations. As we parted Gordon pulled deeply on a short butt of cigarette. He looked me steadily in the eye and told me to be careful. I told him he should wear a mask when he sprays.

The second Chickasaw bluff, once the townsite of Randolph, Tennessee, is thirty-five miles above Memphis. Randolph vied with Memphis in size and importance before the Civil War. But Union General William Tecumseh Sherman burnt the city to the ground. Randolph is no more. All that remains on the river is a casting plant that makes rip-rap for the Army Corps of Engineers.

At the third Chickasaw bluff, seven miles above Memphis, the worst marine disaster of U.S. history occurred. Two weeks after the end of the Civil War some 2,000 Union soldiers were headed upriver on the steamboat *Sultana*. Newly freed from Confederate prisons, the men were weak, sick, wounded and malnourished. The boat was heavily overloaded. It nearly capsized at Helena, Arkansas when a photographer on shore attracted men all to one side. The photograph survives, documentation of the *Sultana's* last day. On April 26, 1865 her boiler exploded and sent more than sixteen hundred men to their watery grave.

The fourth Chickasaw bluff is Memphis.

> *"Aw, naw. I know this place." [He produces a crumpled parchment.] "Here it is on the chart. Look, it says here: 'Continue until you come to the square of the walled town which is the end of the CaMIno ReAL and the beginning of the CaMIno REal. Halt there,' it says 'and turn back, Traveler, for the spring of humanity has gone dry in this place'...*"[60]

Memphis, or someplace close, is where DeSoto met the Mississippi. Though he had no parchment to guide him, he, too, had been told to turn back. Arrived at the river in May 1541, his expedition had been ravaged by mid-winter battles with the Alibamus and the Chickasaw. Already two years in the untracked wilderness, the Spaniards were still seeking gold and riches. They had slogged cross-country from Florida fighting natives the whole way. Metal weapons, armor, crossbows and horses gave DeSoto tremendous military advantage. In a single battle thousands of Alibamu braves had exchanged their lives for less than twenty Spaniards. But the unending warfare was taking its toll. DeSoto's men were clothed in rags and except for the herd of swine they brought with them, without provisions. The winter's hardships fomented discontent. Talk of desertion circulated in the ranks.

DeSoto's method of exploration was quite simple. Through an interpreter he would determine which of the local populations was wealthiest. After reconnoitering with heavily armed cavalry DeSoto would devise a strategy and then order his main column forward. Rich from conquests in Peru, DeSoto had financed the Florida expedition privately. But Spain's king, Charles the Fifth, authorized the undertaking. He named DeSoto Governor and Adelantado, the court's official explorer. In commissioning DeSoto the king enjoined him to read the Requerimento, a kind of Miranda statement of conquest, to any natives before resorting to violence. DeSoto ignored it. He used whatever means necessary to advance. His tactics included capturing hostages, placing chiefs under house arrest, threats, feints, cajolery, and full-scale frontal attacks. Some captives were burned at the stake;

others were mutilated or thrown to vicious greyhounds. Subdued provinces were made to provide food, shelter and to otherwise gratify the conquistadors. Native bearers were bound in chains and loaded with baggage for the entourage. The dogs kept them in order.

If anyone on the Camino is bewildered, come to the Gypsy. A poco dinero will tickle the Gypsy's palm and give her vision.[61]

The province of Quizquiz controlled the site where DeSoto arrived at the Mississippi. The exact location is unknown, but signs of an ancient village have been found south of Memphis in Chucalissa Park. DeSoto's handling of the Quizquiz was fairly representative of his tactics. He entered the town in force, taking as many captives as possible. Most of those captured were women, among them the chief's mother. DeSoto sent word to the chief requesting a parley. The chief demanded that DeSoto first release the captives. In the meantime, some four thousand warriors had surrounded the townsite in battle array. When DeSoto freed the prisoners the chief asked what the Spaniards wanted. DeSoto replied that he was desirous of peace. Since he was only passing through it would be enough for the Quizquiz to abandon their town and provide his men with food while they rested up. The natives did as he asked, granting all his demands. Their tradition had foretold the white man's coming.

It's too unknown for my blood. Man, I seen nothing like it except through a telescope once on a pier on Coney Island. "ten cents to see the craters of the moon!"—And here's the same view in three dimensions for nothing![62]

Memphis' Mud Island masterpiece is a concrete scale replica of the lower Mississippi. Developed with lots of support from the Corps of Engineers, Mud Island is a tourist attraction catch-all featuring a museum, rides, a restored WWII bomber, a small boat harbor and more. The Corps' miniature river is small enough to step over and ends in a swimming pool that represents the Gulf of Mississippi. I walked the model's length trying to get an appreciation for what lay before me on the river. But the reduction in scale was too constraining. I simply could not imagine myself paddling along smaller than a stickpin.

Man, I could use a bed now.—I'd like to make me a cool pad on this Camino now and lie down and sleep and dream of being

with someone—friendly…
   Vacancy here! I got a single bed at the "Ritz men only," a little white ship to sail the dangerous night in.[63]

As during a previous visit, I took a room at Memphis State. Though it was Saturday night and still very early, I was too tired to go out. The heat had worn me ragged as an old flag. With mail to collect at the Post Office and that closed until Monday, I decided to catch up on my sleep. I closed the blinds on the room's only window and adjusted the air conditioner. Stretched out on my bed, my eyes were burning from the sun's brilliant river glare. I determined to sleep until that glare was gone. But my river routine betrayed me. At dawn I was wide awake, restless and unable to stay in bed. I got up and went to church. Afterwards, with no claims on my time, I walked down to Beale Street.

At noon, W.C. Handy Park, the locus of Beale Street, was still asleep. I took a seat amongst the pigeons and began writing a long letter to Margaret. Little by little the street came awake and another day evolved. Panhandlers came by every so often, begging a cigarette, or change. One called me "colonel" because of the broad-brimmed straw hat I wore. Before long a few park regulars were taking seats in the performance square. One brought a pillow, another a thermos. They were prepared to wait for the show, and to stay if it were any good. A man and a woman carried a cooler between them to the bleachers. She took out a box of fried chicken and he took out a new cigar. The panhandlers, in giving way to the newcomers, were working the more distant benches on the park's fringe.

With still no sign of musicians, another stratum of audience filtered into the park. These were single men. By their dapper dress it was obvious they had money. The younger panhandlers seemed to know them. Each dandy soon attracted adherents and conversation. Runners were dispatched to the package store. They returned with cigarettes, brown bag quarts and styrofoam cups. The sponsors held court then, doling cigarettes and dispensing from the brown bags into the white cups.

An unusually conspicuous man walked by with a cockatoo on his shoulder. The Rum Boogie Café and BB King's place began emptying blues out onto the street. The flow of people increased a little in volume, though not in speed. Finally the musicians' set-up men arrived. Cases of drums, amplifiers, microphone pedestals and a spaghetti pile of connecting cable were dumped in the little corner where musicians make their stage. The activity attracted people from the street into the shady parts of the bleachers. They settled in groups like flocks of birds homing to a field of ripe grain. Afternoon's breeze wafted over the stands heady with the smell of liquor. The styrofoam cups, empty now, rocked gently back and forth on the sidewalk. On the park bench next to me a man with an A's cap was sleeping, head back and mouth wide open, oblivious. Guitarists, a bass and a lead, began to warm up. The crowd stirred and got themselves comfortable. The panhandlers moved back into the crowd taking the unfilled and unshaded seats, pleading cigarettes from those already settled. When the music began it was gospel.

> *"For what is the heart but a sort of—"*
> *[He makes a high, groping gesture in the air.]*
> *"—A sort of –instrument!—that translates noise into music, chaos into—order..."*
> *[Abdullah ducks almost to the earth in an effort to stifle his mirth. Gutman coughs to cover his own amusement.]*
> *"—a mysterious order!"*
> *[He raises his voice until it fills the plaza.]*[64]

The Watson Singers, as hosts for the day's performances, opened the show. The group is named for its leader and promoter, a thin middle-aged man of the cloth. The singers, all young and neatly dressed, had come to testify to the Lord. Their first songs were gospel harmonies. The lead singer, a sharp-featured soprano, flourished her phrase endings. As the show progressed she stepped out front, ahead of the chorus and closer to the audience. She had long, brightly painted fingernails and pointed them as she sang, sometimes to herself, to the audience and often to the sky. Her movements were as sudden and sharp as her voice, as though she were trying to puncture something. Gradually she took over even more of the singing, rocking way back on the higher notes, gripping the microphone tightly and making a whip of its cord. By set's end she was the whole show, assailing the mike like it was a tin funnel in a deaf man's ear. Meanwhile Reverend Watson was working the crowd with a plastic bucket, taking donations for the Lord.

The next group, all male, was centered by the Reverend Glass, a big, square sort of man. Glass introduced the lead harmonist as his brother, the drummer as his son, and the accompanying guitarists as his friends. Speaking slowly, with a broad smile, he calmed the audience, preparing them for a less strident show. Telling stories of his origins and childhood Reverend Glass asked how many of his audience had been "raised up" on a farm. Laughing as he measured his audience for recognition of the double entendre he waved his hand to encourage more response. Without singing a note he'd already drawn the day's first "hallelujah." The drummer and bass guitarist used the Reverend's wave as tempo to initiate some background music and a beat. Satisfied that his stage was appropriately set the Reverend closed his eyes, leaned back, and waited for the first chord progression to resolve. Then he began to sing. His baritone voice was deep and wide as the river. His was a work song, a field song, and the very root of gospel and blues. His lyrics were about flyin' tractors in the afternoon's tedious heat, about seeing his brother coming from the opposite way up the field, round after round and standing up and hollering to him "Yeeeeehoa!" And then, when they had each turned at the field's end and were closing toward one another again, how his brother would stand and holler. Here Glass's brother echoed a beautiful, high tenor, clear and incredibly long, "Yeeeeehoa!" Their song developed into a duet and gradually the Reverend coaxed the crowd in on his turn of voice. The performance ended with the brothers and audience, me included, applauding one another. Mr. Watson, for his part, was making the rounds again with his bucket.

The next morning I was on hand when the Post Office opened. From Michigan I got letters, more cookies, and a book of Robert Burns poetry—Margaret's family is Scottish. From home I got a packet of bills. Walking back toward Mud Island I alternated between reading Margaret's letters and at the same time a city map. Before leaving Memphis I wanted to visit the Civil Rights Museum.

> *Well, one of them's come back. He was very thirsty. He found the fountain dry. He started toward the hotel. He was politely advised to advance no further. But he disregarded this advice. Action had to be taken. And now, and now—that old blind woman they call "La madrecita?"—She's come into the plaza with the man called "The Dreamer"...*[65]

The Lorraine Hotel, after having been condemned once by the city, was undergoing restoration in order that it could house the new Civil Rights Museum. Scheduled to open in 1990, the museum was still under construction a year later. The Lorraine had been chosen because Dr. Martin Luther King, Jr. had been assassinated there, on the hotel's balcony, April 4th, 1968. A magazine article the summer of my journey said King's room for that day was being restored in detail that shocked his wife Coretta. Plastic chicken bones replicated the Reverend's last supper. The hotel's outside is not very appealing either. It recalls depreciation profits and strip mall architecture of the sixties. The area near the hotel epitomized urban decay. I was deeply saddened by the whole scene. It did not rekindle for me any of the soaring hopes, goals or dreams that King articulated. Rather, it recalled the hatred he faced, its brutality and ignorance.

Across the street from the hotel a woman had been protesting the museum every day for over four years. She said money spent on the museum should have been spent on poor people. She said Dr. King spelled out how he wanted to be eulogized, in accordance with the eight beatitudes, as a drum major for peace and justice. But what still assaults my memory is not the protestor, nor the museum. The most crushing moment of my deeply moving visit came as I read the plaque outside the compound. The plaque gives reference to Reverend Ralph Abernathy's eulogy for Dr.King. Abernathy took a verse from the Old Testament, "Behold the dreamer cometh. Let us kill him, and then we shall see what becomes of his dream." In 1986 President Ronald Reagan proclaimed Dr. King's January birthday a national holiday. Reagan quoted Dr. King, "We cannot solve this problem through retaliatory violence." Five years later, almost to the day, Reagan's vice-president and successor, George Bush, unleashed Desert Storm. We have surely seen what has become of Dr. King's dream.

There is an eccentric man named Mongo who operates a store on Front Street in Memphis. He's considered a civic embarrassment but was running for mayor the summer I visited. His bizarre platform, posted in the storefront, was illustrated with skunks, tails lifted and spraying. Mongo decries several of the city's recent development projects as wasteful fraud, including Beale Street and Mud Island. He also calls for public executions. But the most notorious scandal he attacked was the downtown's unfinished, giant silver pyramid. The pyramid's primary investor, Mr. Schlenker, skipped town and left the city holding the bag for about $100 million. Mongo said the pyramid was a waste. I agree. The city where Dr. King was shot didn't need a glaring new symbol of opulence, nor such a potent reminder of slavery.

That's the furthest departure a man could make! I guess you're sailing to Athens? There's another war there and like all wars since the beginning of time it can be interpreted as a—struggle for what?[66]

After resting for a few days DeSoto and his men began reconstruction of barges to cross the Mississippi. From the opposite shore thousands of natives watched. A delegation of two hundred canoes was sent to meet the Spaniards. Archers stood erect in the centers of the canoes, flanked on either side by paddlers. Bows, arrows and shields were held ready to defend both paddlers and passengers. The braves were richly painted with ochre, wearing brilliant plumes. Chiefs and sub-chiefs sat at the rear of the larger canoes, shaded beneath awnings. As the deputation approached shore the head chief addressed the Spaniards. He called DeSoto the most powerful lord of the earth and offered obedience and service. DeSoto encouraged the natives to come ashore. Three canoes, filled with loaves of pressed persimmons and fish came to the shore as gifts from the chief. DeSoto thanked the chief and again requested that he land. The natives, growing suspicious, began paddling away from shore. At that moment the Spaniards fired a flight of crossbow bolts and killed several of the delegation. The canoes retreated. For days afterwards the braves would return each day at three in the afternoon to fire a single flight of arrows. Meanwhile the Spaniards were building barges to cross the river. On the day the barges were completed no native canoes came. Next day the Spanish crossed to the other side of the river unhindered. They found the native city of Aquixo abandoned.

The land DeSoto crossed to, north of present day Helena, Arkansas, was extensively cultivated. Fields of maize and orchards of fruit and nut trees separated cities with thousands of inhabitants. Today the area is still heavily agricultural. Cotton is the main crop. King Cotton was born of plantations and slaves in the antebellum Mississippi Delta, the area extending south from Missouri to the Gulf of Mexico. Because cotton growing was so labor intensive Arkansas' plantations used large numbers of slaves. By the Civil War blacks were the most populous race in the Delta. They remain so to this day. At war's end the plantation system was destroyed, and not only for the white landowners. Blacks, though given freedom, had no means to use it. They had no land, no tools, no education and in many cases no family. All they had was a history of perverse relationships with fellow humans and with the earth itself.

I thought it was a disgusting thing to do, to snatch a man's heart from his body! What can a man do with another man's heart?[267]

Modern agriculture in the Delta requires very little labor. Giant tractors till the soil, cropdusters control the weeds and combines replace the many hands that used to pick the cotton. Cropdusting season was in full swing when I paddled through. For days on end I saw planes working fields along the river, pirouetting over the trees like giant dragonflies. One afternoon I walked into a small Delta town hoping to make a phone call. Two young men repairing a pickup told me the only payphone was at a convenience store out on the highway. They were going after an automotive part and offered me a lift. In small talk on the way over the driver mentioned his family's thousand-acre cotton farm. As we pulled up to the gas pumps a black man our age came out of the store. I stepped down thanking the driver for the ride. Before I'd finished the black man was beside me. He nodded howdy and stepped into the cavity of the cab's open door. Addressing the driver he asked for work. The driver told him there was none. The black man asked to be called if any work came up. Then he paid his respects to us all, walked across the highway and tossed a twist-off bottle cap into the weeds as he took his first swig.

DeSoto and his men spent weeks exploring the Mississippi's west bank. Small expeditions were sent to reconnoiter lands to the north and west. The northern expedition was guided by native traders along the route which was later to become known as El Camino Real. Somewhere near Cape Girardeau the traders obtained copper, and more importantly, salt. It was the Spaniard's first salt in months. Everywhere were swamps and backwaters. In Delta country the river constantly loops back on itself and used to frequently change channels. Ensley Bar, Cow Island Bend, Horseshoe Lake, Council Lake, the St. Francis River and the Prairie Point Towhead are today's chartnames for the river's old channels. The bars and towheads, with their miles of sandy beach, display the river's ability to move massive amounts of material. Heat waves across these expansive bars create mirages. Paddling around the river bends I sometimes saw towboats floating above the sand. The shifting and distorting river sand distorts time as well. It has hidden the civilizations DeSoto encountered. Part of Pacaha is thought to have washed into the river's sand-shifting hourglass. The sites of other provinces, Aquixo, Casqui and Quigate are uncertain as well. No maps were kept of DeSoto's forays near the river and the various accounts tell conflicting stories. But those accounts and recent archeological investigation all agree that the west bank of the river from Memphis to Helena was densely populated.

Excuse my ignorance, but what place is this? What is this country and what is the name of this town? I know it seems funny to ask such a question. Loco! But I was so glad to get off that rotten tub that I didn't ask nothing of no one...[68]

Above all, Helena, Arkansas is a river town. The Army Corps of Engineers is working south of town to develop a slackwater commercial harbor. The harbor represents tens of millions of dollars in both materials and labor. Its purpose is to attract barge shipping so that Helena, once a thriving river port, can revive past fortunes. For its part, the state of Arkansas is planning a pleasure craft harbor at Helena to complement the fed's commercial one. The state's project is linked to a larger scheme of attracting river tourists. In addition to the harbor, a riverside park is planned as well. The former railroad station downtown has already been converted to a tourist attraction, the Delta Cultural Center.

More than river improvement is at stake in Helena. The larger purpose for all the projects is Helena's distressed economy. Money spent on the harbor is only a fraction of what's already being spent on welfare payments and housing subsidies. Not including harbor funding, approximately sixty percent of Helena's economy is federal largesse. The huge government expenditures are an attempt to resurrect Helena from entrenched poverty. It is hoped that the mix of tourism and river industry will put the city on its feet. But the people I talked with in Helena wonder whether economic measures are enough.

Mrs. Wanda Ridge is a trustee for Helena's public library and museum. Within minutes of my entry there she had virtually turned over the keys of the city. Helena has not only a rich history, but also people like Mrs. Ridge who are trying to make it more accessible. She telephoned a retired friend to take me on a tour of the area. When I told her I was interested in native history she put me in touch with Mr. Joe Madonia. Later in the day, after I had researched in the library for hours, she invited me to the Ridge home later for a shower and a real bed. Helena's public library is marvelous. It has catalogued, indexed and cross-referenced articles and reminisces of the local historical society for the past one hundred years. As a digression, here is one example of the invaluable river stories the library preserves:

> We have seen all types of river transportation. Possibly the one mode of river traveling that gained the most publicity was done by the man who walked down the river in 1907. He was Professor Charles Oldrieve who walked from Cincinnati to New Orleans, a distance of 1,000 miles. He made his trip during the winter and high water. He wore pontoon shoes of

cedar 4'5" long, 5" wide, and 7" high. His wife accompanied him in a rowboat. He admitted to falling only one time. The professor did the stint on a $5,000 bet. He averaged 25 miles a day.[69]

I looked up Professor Oldrieve's account in New Orleans weeks later and learned that he had indeed successfully completed the trip, though his wife did not. She died of exhaustion within a week of their New Orleans arrival.

Joe Madonia agreed to meet me in the library after work. In the meantime I visited Crowley's Ridge, the only prominent topographic feature this side of the Delta. Crowley's Ridge runs generally north and south between Helena and Bell City, Missouri, a distance of about two hundred miles. As the only high ground of the western Delta the ridge sits well above flood level. Natives favored the ridge for hunting, traveling and for siting their villages. It is likely that the native trade route which evolved into El Camino Real had Crowley's Ridge as its southernmost leg. At the advantageous intersection of both ridge and river Helena was an ideal city site. For Joe Madonia it is the ideal place to follow his lifelong passion, the search for artifacts.

As Joe entered the library he greeted me by pointing out an arrowhead beneath the library's glass counter. He named the roseate point as one he'd found, telling the place, time and weather of its finding. At the sound of his voice a black child stepped out from the stacks. Joe introduced me to Isaac, his artifact-hunting buddy. Bonds of respect and affection between the two were obvious. Isaac squirmed when Joe praised the boy's ability to pick searching places and to find objects. The two talked privately and then Isaac left. Joe said Isaac was too busy with his young friends to hunt artifacts anymore. Joe seemed resigned to losing his partner. At sixty years of age he was poor competition for Nintendo. He knows artifact collection is considered obscure and is unvalued by Isaac's friends. But Joe wants to help young people find treasures in the earth as he does. He wants to help them expand their dimension of time beyond the present. The vignette was a good introduction to Joe and his avocation. He invited me to see his collection.

Joe has over ten thousand artifact specimens mounted and labeled for display. He is well versed in material culture, methods of manufacture, dating and current value. He stays abreast of current legislation affecting the collection and hunting of artifacts. He has grinding stones, pestles, mortars, arrowheads, bird points, drills, hoes, thumb scrapers, palm scrapers, amulets, beads, bolo balls, atlatl weights, crystals, pottery sherds and more. Some pieces are exquisitely manufactured while others are so crude they looked like simple stones to my untrained eye. For Joe each piece became an earthy catalyst of time and memory. For him each piece speaks a story. Joe's eyes and speech reveal more than the objects he handles. He mimes their usage and manufacture. He tells stories of their discovery. The specimens speak through him and he holds them with reverence.

Joe told me practical tips for finding artifacts, the best weather, topography and time of year. He also told me how to record discovery data and obtain permission from landowners. Then he chuckled to himself. When I asked why, he told me another way to find artifacts. "Do you want to know how I really find these things? I pray. I think back as far as I can imagine, letting the day's responsibilities and everything else just fall away, like pieces off a chipped stone. I try to look at the earth and sky like the first people did. I talk to the Great Spirit."

Perhaps prayer achieves some timeless state that fuses the object's finder, its maker, and its user in a single purpose of worked stone. Each artifact is a sum of industry, ingenuity, ability, personality, individuality and patience. Perhaps even love. Joe is an expert in identifying and collecting artifacts because he has learned to pray with the Old Ones. He communes with America's ancestors by finding lost bits of their lives and saving them, by teaching them to Isaac and showing them to me.

The Old Ones of the Mississippi were mound builders. In Chickasaw legend they were a race called Na-hom-lo-tall, a gigantic people from the land of the sunrise. The Old Ones domesticated the woolly mammoth, using them as beasts of burden. In legend the mammoths were herded together to trample the forests and make the vast prairie. Then they were used to build the great mounds revered by later generations. Natives considered the mounds too sacred to disturb. When DeSoto arrived, mounds throughout the Mississippi and Ohio valleys numbered in the thousands. Effigy mounds of snakes, birds, turtles and other animals, burial mounds, all had religious purpose and survived intact for thousands of years. But with the coming of Europeans the mounds were plundered for artifacts. Others were destroyed as land was settled and brought under cultivation. Until the 1990 Graves Protection Act there was little regard for the sacredness of native mounds. Unfortunately the new act came too late for the mounds near Helena. Mounds had been destroyed in building the city and the river levees. Others had been plundered for the Quapaw pottery. Its unique designs and shapes are especially valued. Three sites that had survived earlier onslaughts were excavated with heavy machinery while the Protection Act was being debated, sad proof of its need.

Though Joe would like to make his living finding and exhibiting artifacts his real job is directing Helena's public housing authority. Ostensibly private, most of the authority's funding comes from the federal government. Tenants pay rent with federal funds and operating shortfalls are covered by the feds, too. Joe says one reason for the private façade is so the feds can avoid pension liabilities for employees like him. He's not ready to retire yet in any case. He hopes to curate his collection of artifacts in a museum one day, whether public or private. I treated my new friend to dinner at the Casqui Restaurant just before it closed for the night. Joe indulged in an order of onion rings and I in a piece of pecan pie. His wife hasn't allowed him to eat onion rings since bypass surgery two years ago. "Larrupin' good" he described them, a localism for which not even Joe could give me the origin.

In Spanish accounts a tribe, chief, province and principal village all carried the same identifier, such as Casqui. This may have reflected how intertwined native communities were in understanding their relationship with one another, their tribal rankings and the lands where they lived. On the other hand it may simply have been a convenience for the interpreters. Casqui's capital held over four hundred log and stucco cabins, each occupied by several families. Other large Casqui villages were located on the nearby rivers and backwaters. The chief lived on a high mound in the principal village that was fronted with an apron of land, a sort of courtyard where it's thought that his wives and attendants lived. The Casqui, like Aquixo and Quizquiz were numerous and powerful. But all were vassals to Pacaha, a province several miles north. In a long history of conflict Casqui had been made submissive to Pacaha. Pacaha's dominance and superiority was reflected in the capital. Its outer stockade of logs enclosed the city and a large public plaza. Within the plaza was a temple and within the temple were the bones of Pacaha's ancestors. A moat, connected to the Mississippi, separated the city's island fortress where the chief lived. Fish were penned within the moat and its water level was regulated by a system of weirs. The fortress, complete with towers, held some five hundred cabins. Yet there was an even greater city than this. DeSoto's party encountered the largest city of their expedition at Quigate. That city was divided into three wards, with the highest being a mound where the chief lived. It is thought that Quigate, most magnificent of all the native cities, was located near the present site of Helena.

For new companions are not as familiar as old ones but all the same—they're old ones with only slight differences of face and figure, which may or may not be improvements, and it would be selfish of me to be lonely alone...[70]

Joe offered to take me to the Ridges' when we were finished with dinner. On the way over I asked him to stop by the grocery store so I could get some toothpaste and shampoo. I put it down to his age when he stayed in the car with the motor running. The store was like a thousand others, plate glass windows fronting a row of checkouts and in back of them aisles of stocked shelves. An enclosed and elevated service island guarded the entrance. There were the usual splashy displays of merchandise and promotional ads. I located the few items I needed and headed back to the checkout counter.

The store was nearly empty and only one checker was working. The single other customer was in front of me, a very obese black woman. She was splay-footed, wore floral pink shorts and a faded cranberry tanktop. Her facial features, round as her figure, made her eyes seem unnaturally depressed. A baby about four years old and wiry as a telephone cord clutched the woman's legs. With her free hand the child ran her fingers over candies and gum in the display slots. The woman purchased corn curls and a carton of soda, paying with food stamps. The child stared up at me. As the checker made change a thin black man stepped into the checkout lane. His attire was nondescript except for a pair of neon-green plastic sunglasses promoting a brand of cigarettes. He'd already made a purchase, a six-pack of beer, and was waiting. When the checker offered the woman's change he grabbed it with his free hand and then hastened to the exit.

As my items were being checked the store manager stepped up into the elevated service island. He took a stool at the window and pivoted slightly to face the store's exit. A leather harness spanned his white shirt across the back. I assumed it supported a prosthesis. Curious, I turned at the door as I was leaving. I saw then that the harness holstered a large nickel-plated pistol.

DeSoto left deserted Aquixo and entered Casqui with the advantage of surprise. The Casqui received him in peace. The chief called DeSoto "Son of the Sun, Very High, Powerful and Renowned master." He begged DeSoto to restore sight to two blind men and to make it rain.

Wanda and Gene Ridge run two small Helena grocery stores in partner with Gene's twin sister and husband. The stores are located near the housing projects Joe Madonia runs. Both couples were waiting up to talk with me about my trip. We talked about the river, about their city and about life in general. Both couples had new grandchildren to brag about, born within days of each other. Both couples were concerned about their community. They see no end to the poverty. They see a welfare system that maintains but doesn't heal. As grocers, their success depends on supplying items their customers want. Their customers buy compulsively with little regard for nutrition or economy. The poor spending habits are passed on from generation to generation. The Ridges, like Joe Madonia, are concerned about the young people in Helena.

The next morning I went with Wanda to one of the family grocery stores. A simple, block-lettered, black and white metal sign spanned the storefront, "REEVE'S GROCERY." The entrance was a screen door that closed with a coil spring. To its right was a single display window. It was laced with cyclone fencing to prevent burglaries. Inside the store was dark, musty and spare. There was no piped-in music, no overhead fluorescent lighting and no nested bungle of shopping carts. The floor was old and wooden. The shelving was the same. Four islands and the walls held all the merchandise in the store. Barely ten steps long the islands were closed on the ends as though to hide their meager supplies.

The opposite front corner of the store was squared off by a meat counter. A single bare incandescent bulb hung from three feet of wire rooted in the high ceiling. The bulb was backlight to a glass-fronted display case that had a single shelf above a low bottom. The meat was mostly packages of cold cuts. The only exceptions were a tray of pork knuckles and an immense tray of bacon. The bacon filled the display's bottom like a hog that had been run sideways twice through a bread slicer. I selected a box of minute rice, a bag of raisins and a bunch of bananas and then carried them to the check out. Wanda's brother-in-law sat at the register behind the counter. He rang my purchase and bagged my goods. We shook hands goodbye as I pulled the door open. The outside thermometer read ninety-two degrees. Wanda took me back to the river.

Casqui had been without rain and the crops were dying when DeSoto arrived. The suddenness of his arrival, his incredible horses and superior weapons, the different color of his skin, his totally strange language and confident attitude all marked him as a messenger of God. The Casqui asked DeSoto to petition his obviously powerful Spanish God for rain. DeSoto ordered a giant cross to be erected from the largest cypress trees that could be found. The cross took more than one hundred men to move. It was placed on the highest mound in the city so that it could be seen for a great distance. Modern archeologists have found remains of a large, charred, cypress post in a mound north of Helena. The Casqui wailed to DeSoto because the Spaniards were so long in making preparations. Over fifteen thousand natives took part in the ceremony that DeSoto's priests finally conducted. They joined in the singing, brought up their afflicted and showed great faith in the Spanish God. That night a heavy rain began to fall. It continued for two days.

French explorers passed through the area near Helena less than one hundred and fifty years after DeSoto. Armadas of canoes did not greet them, they saw no great cities, or temples and very few people. Archeologists assume that disease spread by the Spaniards devastated the native populations. They hypothesize that survival rates of less than one percent extinguished the great civilizations, the Pacaha, Quizquiz, Aquixo, Casqui and Quigate. But hard evidence to substantiate disease epidemics has not been found. The hard fact is simply that those civilizations disappeared.

I was paddling away from Helena's landing when two men a little ways further downstream hailed me from a pontoon boat. They cut their engine and waited until I paddled alongside. They asked if I wanted a ride. I assumed they meant a ride out to the main channel. But their intention was for me to tie onto their craft and join them under the boat's canopy. I was only too happy to oblige. The two, brothers, were wonderful entertainment all that day. The elder called their sightseeing trip a dream. The younger brother allowed as how it was a dream all right, a nightmare really. The younger brother tried to enlist me in his mutiny. He'd enlisted his elder brother earlier but somehow things just didn't work out. Most amazing was the elder brother's continual referral to his pet pig. I found out later that "pet pig" was his nickname for his wife.

Helena, or Quigate, was the last stop on El Camino Real. DeSoto died of fever, probably malaria, a year after he first saw the Mississippi. He was returning to the river from the west never having found any gold. His followers buried him quietly, fearful of letting the natives know their leader was gone. Then another fear overtook them. They became convinced that the natives would exhume DeSoto's body and desecrate it. So they exhumed it themselves, took it to the deepest part of the river, weighted it with sand and sunk it. The local chief was not deceived by all their precautions. He offered them two maidens to accompany DeSoto on his voyage to the spirit world. The Spaniards declined his offer. They told him that DeSoto had gone to visit the sun and would soon return.

DeSoto came to the Mississippi as an early harbinger of the European migration. The native civilizations that he encountered could not withstand the power of his sword. Perhaps in some similar way Dr. Martin Luther King's words herald the coming of a new civilization as well. Dr. King often talked of nonviolence being the sword that heals. Dr. King also understood the powerful imagery of the river. He was known to quote the prophet Amos, "Let justice run down like waters and righteousness like a mighty stream."

I hear him often. I hear his words like the high calling of a brother still working the hot fields of our troubled country. Still working though he has left our confused Road of Souls to take his place on the King's Highway.

Feu de Joie

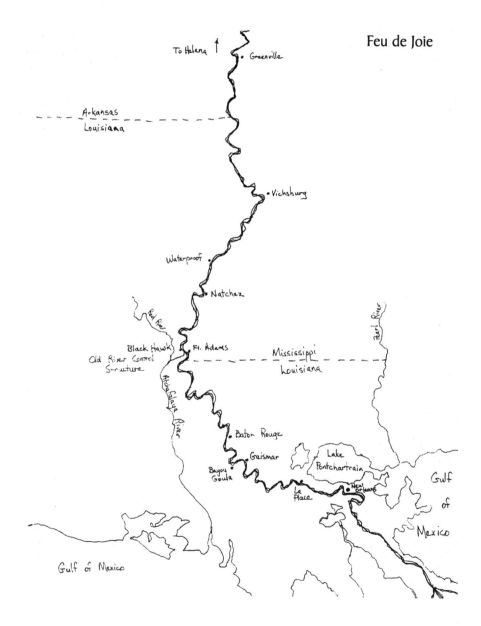

To Helena •Greenville

Arkansas
Louisiana

•Vicksburg

Waterproof•

•Natchez

Red River

Black Hawk Ft. Adams
Old River Control
Structure

Mississippi
Louisiana

Pearl River

Atchafalaya River

•Baton Rouge

•Geismar

Bayou
Goula

Lake
Pontchartrain

Gulf
of
Mexico

La
Place

•New
Orleans

Gulf of Mexico

Feu de Joie

By late August I was guiding my impossibly small and frail canoe through the final river expanses of Louisiana. The high summer Mississippi pours its way into bayou country like a glaring heat of molten steel. It bores serpentine paths through the surrounding country, dissolving it into long, brilliant, shimmering wet mirages. During those last intensely hot afternoons willow groves on the banks above the revetment were my oasis. I would lay beneath the gentle trees, waiting for the heat to pass, idling in the fragrant shade. The willows' wispy branches, pendant with narrow leaves, would sweep back and forth in the wind like bird's tongues chattering to the sand. Occasionally I'd doze off. Sometimes, startled awake, I'd rouse abruptly, sensing some great urgency, disoriented by endless feverish days. It seemed like the earth was turning away without me. The river willows in Louisiana have thick masses of root-like tendrils sprouting from their trunks well above ground level. These clumpish secondary root systems dangle like long, black dreadlocks six feet or more above the ground. I'd waken with the willows leaning over me as though in council, waiting for me to get up. Their dreadlocks would be gently swaying and the narrow leaves clicking calmly in the breeze.

"A raindrop falling in Lake Itasca would arrive at the gulf in about ninety days." So says a sign at the Mississippi headwaters. Sitting on the steps of St. Patrick's Church in Fort Adams, Louisiana, I was content to let the drop gain on me a little. Some eighty days into my journey, New Orleans was now less than a week away. Margaret and I had talked about getting together there when I finished. I had hoped to phone her and perhaps arrange that we could meet and celebrate. Two miles of dirt road had led from the river to this tiny hamlet. There was a public phone mounted outside the general store. Unfortunately the store was closed and I had no change.

Determined to make change with some coin-laden resident I settled on the church steps to wait. It was late afternoon and though still very warm, the day's heated edge had passed. Pecans falling from a nearby tree dropped onto a corrugated metal roof. As each one fell its sharp report dissolved in the languid surroundings. The nuts themselves would roll a little ways down the roof, find a slot and rest. Theirs was the only noise in the village. While waiting for a passerby I wrote a letter to Margaret, the final entry in my river journal. It was a long, slow, drawling, Mississippi gumbo of a missive. The dropping pecans suggested phase endings and the town itself a theme.

Shuttered clapboard lodges of private hunt clubs line one side of the Fort Adams' commons. The commons is primarily a place to park pickups convenient to the general store. A set of hanging scales, roofed over and slabbed beneath with concrete, flanks the dirt road and one side of the square. Angled for effective view, in a few months the sheltered scales would be heavy with display. Bears and venison, run by hounds and shot in the cane breaks, would be rated on these public instruments. Though contested in the field, here in the public square is where justice would be made. Here the fortunes of shooters could be accurately measured. Directly opposite the road, completing the square, stands the general store. On its veranda are vending machines for ice and soda. Tacked all round on the unpainted plywood walls were notices and informational flyers. An election was coming up. One prominent poster said "MAKE A CROSS FOR JIM BUCK ROSS." Another pecan dropped onto the metal roof and in the distance a hound began to bell. Mosquitoes were harassing me to leave. Reluctantly, after nearly two hours with no one yet about, I did.

Fort Adams lies just opposite and below the Old River Control Structure and Black Hawk's Bend. In recent years the Army Corps of Engineers has spent billions controlling the Mississippi hereabouts. The river is seeking a new channel, one further west along the Atchafalaya basin. But the Corps, by building the control structure, is preventing the river from abandoning Baton Rouge and New Orleans. The Army wants to keep the river right where it is. They weren't always so accommodating. Fort Adams was abandoned by both the Army and the river. Once an important frontier post, its last garrison was pulled out in 1819. Not long afterwards the river pulled out, too. It meandered to a channel two miles further west and stayed there. Instead of trying to stop it or follow it Fort Adams' residents simply built a dirt road, the same one I walked into town.

Walking back to the river my dusty tracks were just as I had made them. No one but me had passed. Seeing so many footprints, seeing them wind away from the river, I began to realize how far I had come. Yet, on the whole, the land was very like Minnesota at the river's headwaters. Both places absorbed human activity with a sense of barely tamed wilderness. I noticed again tree blinds for ambushing deer. Spaced at even distances along the road, they held good vantage over the broad savannas leading down to the river. Occasional drives, barred across and signed against trespass, emphatically proclaimed lands reserved for private hunting. Most of the drives led uphill into modest bluffs, away from the river. Some ended in clusters of buildings, seasonal camps. Spare, weather-beaten cabins marked them, mostly overgrown and vacant. A few were surrounded by clotted nests of wire dog kennels. One compound, typical of them all, was centered by its turnout. A yard light burned above the circular drive though it was not yet dusk. Below the light, standing one-armed and ramrod-straight, was an old iron pump.

Back at the landing, men were limbing out a fallen tree. Its massive trunk had been struck by lightning and was an explosion of twisted shards. The canopy, though mostly intact, lay incongruously on its side, like the crown of a fallen monarch. Six-foot long splinters littered the ground. Other splinters angled outward from the wrecked core, protruding on all sides. The men worked slowly. They paused after each cut discussing the tree's puzzle. Broken high, parts of the tree were still under tension. Much of its weight was still dangerously far above the ground. In logging jargon the tree was a "widow maker." One of the men, turning his head sideways, spit a thick brown stream of tobacco juice. His partner lit a cigarette. Then, between them, they hoisted a log and carried it uphill to a waiting pickup. I saw the log's end, yellow swirled with dark brown rings, unmistakably pecan. They heaved the severed branch sideways into the truck's bed and I watched it roll forward to the pickup's cab. Sounds and the evening's colors seemed muted, sepia-toned. It was as though the dust at my feet had absorbed them. After a moment, the chainsaw began again.

A frightful thunderstorm suddenly arose: Lightning struck their temple, burned all their idols, and reduced their temple to ashes. Immediately the savages ran out in front of their temple making terrible shrieks, tearing out their hair, and raising their arms aloft. Facing their temple, they invoked their Great Spirit, like men possessed, to extinguish the fire; then they seized dirt and smeared it on their bodies and their faces. Fathers and mothers brought their children and strangled them and cast them into the fire.[71]

Penicaut recorded the above spectacle in 1704 at a Tensas village near the present town of Waterproof, Louisiana. For me, the Tensas' terrible fear of lightning, if not their actions, was understandable. Extremely violent storms, even hurricanes, are part of the lower river's weather patterns. In late summer subtropical storms find their way from the Gulf of Mexico up the Mississippi Valley. During the last days of my journey showers spawned by these weather systems were respite from the oppressive southern heat and humidity. Nearly every evening found me paddling in the rain. Less often, twice, the storms brought lightning and violent winds. Once I was made to fear for my life.

It had become my custom to camp on the Mississippi's open sand bars. These bars, up to half a mile wide, extend almost the entire length of the lower river. They shift from bank to bank, always inside and opposite the river's bends. Offering convenience to the river, relief from mosquitoes and truly magnificent sunsets these bars argued against seeking more protected shelter. One typical afternoon, thunderheads began building above the western horizon of the river. Hoping to meet that day's standard mileage quota I continued paddling. The sky gradually filled with clouds, turned gray and lowered. Then, in eerie quiet that harkened a truly violent storm, the clouds took on a bruised, olive hue. I paddled to the nearest bank, an open sand bar, and set my tent in the lee of a drifted tree trunk. Many of these trunks lay stranded on the lower river. Rounding bends one sees them beached like whales on the sandbars, unmoving. Shorn smooth of branches or bark, bleached white by the sun, these nomads wander at the river's pleasure. Some, too waterlogged to float, gradually attract a burial of sand. Others, the passengers, are deposited like this one was, at ports of the river's choosing. This trunk's roots had been turned so often on the river's bottom that only a bulbous knob remained. Tapering from the knob to an abrupt and pointed end the trunk's symmetry suggested a man's cane.

I was eating chocolate pudding from a plastic carton in my tent when the first winds came. They were so violent and sudden that the fragile shelter collapsed immediately. Its stakes lost their sandy purchase and the poles became useless spars tethered to nothing. My own weight was the tent's only anchor. The wind, carrying sand gathered all down the mile-long beach, drove furiously into the flapping tent's hysteric fabric. Beneath the wind's gritty howl I could hear my canoe scraping across the beach, being crabbed toward the river. I gathered the tent about me, gradually wadding it beneath one arm and then emerged from its door like a snake shedding its own skin. Blowing sand, thick in the air, made it difficult to see or breathe, so I pulled my shirt up over my face. Still clutching the tent, I crawled toward the canoe. Sand bit at my bare skin and tore at the tent like a rabid dog. I pushed the canoe alongside the drifted trunk, then lashed them together. Working blindly in the sandstorm I erected the tent again, tying it off to the trunk and canoe. As I finished big drops of rain began falling, settling the blowing sand. Their tattoo accelerated steadily, crescendoing to a sustained deluge. Thoroughly chastened, I crawled back inside the tent. Encrusted with sand and miserable, I resolved never to be caught in the open again.

Several camps later I admired a towering sunset before turning in for the night. This time my canoe was secure and I'd pitched my tent well up the bank in a stand of trees. With nightfall I listened as the wind came into the branches. Like thunderbirds taking roost, cacophonous sweeps of lightning clawed the grove. Waves of electric fire rolled over the river, breaking open the darkness with vehement, jagged arcs. The earth literally shook, resounding with impact from the crashing bolts and branches. A little rain fell wetting the fabric, making it translucent. Sticks and leaves clung to the tent's outside walls as though in fright. They cast portentous shadows, signs that the firmament was failing. Sitting up I watched myself tremble, lit by the unsteady flashes. I was really scared, a pale form, unfamiliar and ghostly. This time there was nowhere for me to go and nothing to do but pray.

The long summer on the river, and the heat, were taking their toll on me. One morning I hiked half a mile across swamp and bramble and then two miles down the levee road into Lake Providence, Louisiana. I saw my first cypress tree on the way in with the curious roots reaching upwards like curled toes. It was Sunday and I needed drinking water, a chance to stretch my legs and the community of church. In town I took a picture of three young boys out picking aluminum cans. One of them asked me how to spell "church." The flashing sign above the bank across the street may have prompted his question. "CH...CH WHAT'S

MISSING? UR." I also bought some tobacco for rolling cigarettes. I hadn't smoked the whole trip, but my resolution was failing. Heading back to the river I tried to take a shorter, more direct route. My canoe waited at the far end of a bayou where a young man was fishing from an old wooden rowboat. I asked for a lift and he obliged, using a piece of lumber as an oar. As payment I traded half the tobacco. But I must have left the rucksack open. Or perhaps earlier, coming back from town, I'd left it open. Gone were my wallet, checkbook, toothbrush and razor.

For the Tensas people fear of lightning was based in tribal belief. They, like most tribes of the lower Mississippi, had a cosmology centered on fire. For them the sun, lightning and fire were all manifestations of the Great Spirit. This belief organized both their lives and their society. Communities and tribal affiliations were identified by the source of temple fires. Villages that shared a common fire were considered a united people.

> From my conversations with the guardians of the temple, I discovered that they acknowledged a supreme being, whom they called Coyococop-Chill, or Great Spirit. The Spirit infinitely great, or the Spirit by way of excellence. The word chill, in their language, signifies the most superlative degree of perfection, and is added by them to the word which signifies fire, when they want to mention the Sun; thus Oua is fire, and Oua-Chill is the supreme fire, or the Sun; therefore, by the word Cyocop-Chill they mean spirit that surpasses other spirits as much as the sun does common fire.[72]

However inconsistently described, the outline above describes essentials of Natchez tribal beliefs. The Natchez were close allies of the Tensas, though of a separate fire. They were masters of the lower river, respected for their power and culture by other tribes as well as the Europeans. Like many river tribes they built mounds and temples. French accounts of Natchez ceremonies offer a glimpse of how mounds, temples and chiefs figured in native worship on the lower Mississippi.

> The sun was their deity; their great chief was called by the same name, and he, in turn, called the sun his brother. Every morning at dawn, attended by his retinue, the chief ascended a mound to converse with his celestial brother. As soon as the sun appeared in the heavens, the chief saluted with a long

howl, and then waved his hand from east to west, and directed what course he should traverse![73]

The relationship between the Natchez chief and the sun is striking, both being considered deities. The Natchez chief was accorded earthly treatment in keeping with his supreme status. All manner of ceremony, dress, food, housing and personal relations showed great deference to him. A similar reverence was accorded to the sun and its manifestation on earth, the eternal fire. Natchez societal hierarchy revolved around the chief and the eternal fire, the brothers. Subchiefs, Suns, ranked below the Great Sun. They and other retainers, including wives and children, formed the ruling class. Commoners formed the lower class. The two classes spoke different dialects, words and speech reinforcing the hierarchy. Nevertheless, there was mobility between the classes both structured and otherwise. Hereditary rights to the Sun class dissolved in the seventh generation. Alternately, those who showed promise in the lower class could advance within the hierarchy. One manner of advancement was to demonstrate ability in learning tribal traditions and ceremonies.

It's worthwhile to note that the French who observed the Natchez were themselves subjects of a Sun King. Louis XIV, also known as Louis the Great, reigned from 1643 until 1725. His adopted title was the "Sun King." He is best remembered for building the palace at Versailles. While the Great Sun of the Natchez built nothing comparable, his village was marked by a prominent temple. Temples were the grand edifices of the lower Mississippi. They varied in size and form depending on tribal affiliation and the wealth of the community. Typical temples were marked by carved totems or painted shells mounted on posts outside their entrance. Some were no more than huts, indistinguishable from common living quarters. The main temple of the Natchez however, was much grander than those of the neighboring tribes. Penicaut, a carpenter and one of the first Europeans to see the Natchez temple, described a round hall thirty feet high, several thousand feet square with walls nearly twenty feet thick. Others described it more modestly. In every case, however, an eternal fire is attested.

> The Natchez have neither sacrifices, libations, nor offerings: their whole worship consists in preserving the eternal fire, and this the Great Sun watches over with peculiar attention.[74]
> In this temple they keep a fire burning continuously. They say this fire represents the sun, which they worship. That is

why they make a fire before the door every morning at sunrise and every evening at sunset. The wood with which they feed the ever-burning fire within the temple has to be oak or walnut from which the bark has been stripped.[75]

Penicaut's reference to walnut trees was generically ambiguous. By way of explanation he enumerated the several varieties of walnuts, giving also his preference.

They have three kinds of walnut trees: there are some that bear nuts as big as one's fist; from these they make bread for their soup. But the best are scarcely bigger than one's thumb; these they call pacanes.[76]

The pecan is actually a type of hickory tree, once unique to the lower Mississippi. The other Natchez fuel Penicaut mentions, oak, may have been the live oak. Live oaks are evergreen, often very old and can grow to immense size. In Bayou Goula, downstream of Fort Adams and just south of Baton Rouge, I met Ivy Stewart. He introduced me to live oaks and together we toured his neighborhood, Bayou Goula.

Ivy grew up with six brothers in a three-room cottage. Just down the road were two live oaks, family heirlooms of a sort. Ivy said a tree expert had aged them at over three hundred years. Tradition passed down from his great-great-great-grandfather held the oaks as mile-markers. They were planted to mark the distance from...well, nowadays no one remembers. As a boy, his refuge was the trees. We stood dwarfed beneath their outstretched arms as he fondly reminisced about days spent climbing them. Once he had filched tomatoes from a neighbor's garden and hidden them in the tree's limbs. After school he had climbed into the leaves and there, unnoticed by the world, he'd eaten his afternoon treats.

Ivy has a master's degree in Agricultural Economics. Though most farms near Bayou Goula are planted to sugar cane, his few acres are sown with soybeans. Big operations like Spiller's Plantation, the Troxclairs', and Messinas' have capital and economies of scale able to handle sugar cane's two-year growth cycle. Smaller operators like Ivy have to use their land differently. While touring the area Ivy talked about sugar and its economics, the bayou and its people. Pointing to a pickup turning off the highway ahead of us he said, "That's Orville Troxclair and his brother Ervin in the seat beside him. They're big sugar growers. See this road—Troxclair—named for 'em. They're the only ones allowed to live on that road. Across the river they got a pond and they're the only ones can fish in it."

Everywhere in the bayou people waved at Ivy. He seemed to know them all by name. Once a sheriff's deputy, he'd also served a term on the school board. In Dorseyville he hailed a woman and at her answer he stopped the car. She asked after his family and why were we riding around in the middle of the day. Leaning over Ivy's door her generous bosom filled the window. It was framed there like a close-up view of bayou scenery. While they small-talked, I looked out the passenger's side. The village was an haphazard collection of shotgun houses. Chickens ran free in the nearest yard. One, a bandy rooster, leapt the road ditch, crowed, and began picking gravel beside our car. My eye fell on a pipe jutting sideways into the ditch. White and plastic, it was dripping a dark gray slime. The ditch was full of sewage. Ivy says the slow, quiet ways of the bayou are changing. That's why these days he sells cars. Shot in the arm over cocaine, he quit his job as deputy sheriff.

Bayou Goula is named for the tribe that peopled the village when the French came, the Bayougoula. They were one of seven small tribes known collectively as the Muskogean. René Robert Cavelier Sieur De La Salle, in his several voyages to the Gulf, met and fought with various of the tribes. In 1686 he sailed from France in an attempt to colonize the mouth of the Mississippi. Meanwhile, Henri De Tonti, LaSalle's right hand man, paddled from Illinois by canoe to rendezvous with him. Tonti, reaching the area, found no sign of LaSalle so he left a letter with a Muskogean chief. A historical marker outside Bayou Goula commemorates the letter. The chief handed it, unopened and perfectly preserved, to Pierre Le Moyne Sieur D'Iberville, the founder of New Orleans, fourteen years later. It read as follows:

> Sir, having found the column on which you placed the arms of France overthrown by driftwood floating downstream, I caused a new one to be erected about seven leagues from the sea, where I left a letter suspended from a tree. All the nations have sung the calumet. These people greatly fear us since your attack on their village. I close by saying it gives me great uneasiness to be obliged to return under the misfortune of not having found you. Two canoes have examined the coast thirty leagues toward Mexico and twenty-five towards Florida.

Unfortunately, LaSalle never got the letter. His own men had assassinated him.

The Bayougoula disappeared. Wars with other tribes, sacrificial killings and colonization ended them. Early colonists were fickle in their relations with bayou natives. Tonti's letter, though short, details how the French equivocated regarding the tribes. Depending on their current need, the French were both ally and enemy, sometimes simultaneously. They smoked the calumet with the same tribes whose members were elsewhere held in bondage. Native slaves worked beside others brought from the Carribean islands, suffering fate in common with them. Punitive expeditions to control slave revolts decimated native populations as well. Incredibly, memory of the Bayougoula lingers on the river. Ivy knew the whereabouts of a native burial ground. He offered to take me there.

Ivy said we were going to a place known as Back-of-Bayou-Goula. We drove for half an hour down gravel roads making turns so often I lost my bearings. The land is flat and level, but distances are concealed. Fields high with sugar cane narrow the road to a jungle path. A crop dusting plane crossed within yards of our windshield, roaring past, gunning its throttle to climb and turn for another pass. It had buzzed us with no warning, so low I could almost read the brand name on the pilot's sunglasses. Ivy knew the pilot, what he was spraying and whose crop was being dusted. None of that knowledge gave me comfort. I was becoming uneasy.

We stopped at what appeared to be a traditional cemetery. Grave markers, more or less in rows, pitched at odd angles through tall grass and patches of weeds. Ivy pointed beyond them to a dry creek bed bordered on either side by trees. Kudzu vine hung like a green pall, blocking view beyond the cemetery's edge. I walked slowly toward the trees, past headstones illegible with age. I was anxious about walking into the creek bed, afraid really. Stopping to read a marker I suddenly felt something biting my legs. Wearing shorts and a pair of sandals I looked down to see ants swarming my calves, ankles and insteps. I'd stepped on a nest of fire ants. No one needed to tell me that they're named for their inflammatory sting. I literally hotfooted it back to the car. Ivy, in cowboy boots and slacks, seemed positively amused. "Sure you don't you want to see those Indian graves?" he kept repeating as we drove away. I'm not sure there were any.

Fire ants, like the kudzu vine, are imports to bayou country. The ants were originally from South America, while kudzu came from Asia. Both are as prevalent and persistent as they are unwelcome. Driving back toward the river we passed a railroad freight car that Ivy's great grandad had converted to a juke joint, the Dew Drop In. It, too, was overgrown with kudzu and when he asked if I wanted to see the inside I just scratched my legs.

For my final few days on the river I was a nameless nomad, drifting like a river snag shorn of roots and branches. Without my wallet I had no cash, no credit cards and no ID. Though I'd made arrangements to have card replacements mailed to New Orleans I wasn't hopeful on that score either. My previous experience picking up General Delivery had shown that postmasters, like bankers, shared a general suspicion of people without ID. I was worn out physically as well. The ant bites and my other cuts and scratches developed localized infections. Little pimples spread over my legs like a mild case of acne. I was exhausted, often feeling woozy and feverish yet rarely able to sleep. The constant sun and heat made me concerned for my health and anxious to finish.

The river, too, seemed weary, surreal and overrun. Ocean tankers and grain ships worked upriver and down moving at speed to navigate the channel. The water was becoming increasingly and obviously more polluted. Thick green moss covered the rocks at water line. The river stank. Not the damp, funky smell I'd grown accustomed to, but something sharper and more pungent, petrochemicals. Ten miles downriver from Bayou Goula, on the opposite bank, is Geismar, Louisiana. South from this point on the river scenery becomes unnatural in the extreme. Pipes suspend from loading derricks alongside barge docks at the river's edge. Behind the docks a network of valves and mains race over the levee and back into miles of flaming incinerator stacks. Here, where the river approaches its greatest volume, it endures its greatest dosage of poisons. The harsh reality is that if the river didn't carry away the poisons, the plants here could not exist.

> More than 400 million pounds of toxic chemicals, including millions of pounds of known or suspected cancer-causing chemicals were discharged last year by 38 plants in Louisiana's industrial corridor...[77]
>
> ...a Shell chemical plant produces...hydrochloric acid, ammonia and sulphuric acid. Next to it stands a Vulcan Materials facility that makes chlorinated solvents.
>
> Less than a mile down the road BASF Wyandotte produces caustic potash, formaldehyde, phosphoric acid, 2,4-dinitrotoluene, phosgene, and other hazardous compounds.
>
> Not far away are facilities operated by Exxon, Shell, Texaco, Gulf, Marathon, Occidental and other oil companies as well

as Dupont, Union Carbide, American Cyanamid, Monsanto, Dow, Stauffer, Allied and other chemical firms.

Nowhere in the nation is there a greater concentration of petrochemical plants than along the 80 mile portion of the Mississippi River known as the "chemical corridor" or "cancer alley."

Among the suspected effects of the chemicals: a concentration of miscarriages among pregnant women and elevated levels of bladder, rectal and lung cancers among all residents.[78]

The petrochemical plants are attracted to the river by its ability to dilute toxic effluent into parts per billion at ratios that satisfy environmental laws. In doing so the river carries not only its own deadly tonic, but it pours a continuous poison cocktail into the Gulf of Mexico as well. The lower river as a pallbearer has gruesome parallel in its own history. The following describes a Natchez funeral, that of a high caste woman.

> The unfortunates, doomed to death, danced while kinsmen of the Dead One sang. When they started off, two by two, in that grand funeral procession, the Dead One was brought from her house, four savages carrying her on their shoulders as on a stretcher. As soon as she was brought forth, the house was set on fire—that is the grand fashion with nobles. The fathers, with the dead children out on their hands, marched in front at intervals of four paces, and after taking ten steps they dropped the children to the ground. Those carrying the Dead One walked on top of these children and three times marched around them. The fathers gathered them up and then fell back in line; and every ten steps they repeated this frightful ritual till they came to the temple, so that the children were mangled in pieces by the time the funeral procession got there.
>
> This nation follows this execrable ritual to this day, in spite of all that has been done to dissuade them.[79]

There are other less industrial evocations of lower river natives than toxins and pollution. New Orleans jazz funerals are an obvious parallel and those processions are anything but morbid. Mardi Gras, happier yet and the hallmark of New Orleans, openly remembers native influence. Masking as an Indian is still a popular way to celebrate. Ironically, the natives of the lower Mississippi were themselves maskers. Whiteface, a longstanding Mardi Gras tradition, was practiced by natives in the dance of the calumet. Nominally Christian today, Mardi Gras came to New Orleans with the city's founder, D'Iberville. The holiday began in Greece as a vernal celebration. Romans appropriated it in the form of a month long orgy that climaxed in the "Festival of Joy," a day when laws were largely abandoned. The church, as antidote, instituted Carnival, the farewell to flesh ending in Mardi Gras, Fat Tuesday.

While Mardi Gras retains hints of native practices and ceremonies, popular folklore of the lower Mississippi has even stronger ties to native legends and characters. Several Natchez stories highlight a prominent native archetype, Rabbit. The following story is titled "Rabbit Steals Fire."

> All of the people came together and said: "How shall we obtain fire?" It was agreed that Rabbit should try to obtain fire for the people. He went across the great water to the east. He was received gladly, and a great dance was arranged. Then Rabbit entered the dancing circle, gaily dressed, and wearing a peculiar cap on his head into which he had stuck four sticks of rosin. As the people danced they approached nearer and nearer the sacred fire in the center of the circle. The Rabbit also danced nearer and nearer the fire. The dancers began to bow to the sacred fire, lower and lower. Rabbit also bowed to the fire, lower and lower. Suddenly, as he bowed very low, the sticks of rosin caught fire and his head was a blaze of flame. The people were amazed at the impious stranger who had dared to touch the sacred fire. They ran at him in anger, and away ran Rabbit, the people pursuing him. He ran to the great water and plunged in, while the people stopped on the shore. Rabbit swam across the great water, with the flames blazing from his cap. He returned to his people, who thus obtained fire from the east.[80]

One wonders if the rabbit archetype of Natchez stories is connected somehow with Br'er Rabbit stories of Uncle Remus. Both originate in the South, and rosin is close enough to tar. It seems only a short hop from the Rabbit of the Natchez to Br'er Rabbit in Uncle Remus. Might the common experience of slavery have born tarbaby and Br'er Rabbit from the rosin sticks of "Rabbit Steals Fire?"

Here is another Natchez legend of Rabbit called "The Rescue of the Sun."

An old woman put the sun into an earthen pot and kept it there. Rabbit wanted it and stayed at her house dancing. Rabbit said to the people assembled, "Sing for me so that I can dance." "We don't know how to sing for you," they answered. "Sing 'Rabbit, Rabbit, Rabbit'," he said. So they sang "Rabbit, Rabbit, Rabbit" and he danced. While he was dancing, he said, "Move it toward me," and they moved it toward him. Again he said, "Move it toward me. I am dancing like a crazy person." After they had moved it toward him farther, he seized the sun. They chased him as he ran away but he kept on with it. On the way he struck the pot repeatedly against the bushes but it did not break, so again he took it and ran on. Then he struck it against a hornbeam tree and broke it in pieces.

Then all the creatures assembled and counseled, and all the flying things gathered together. They wanted to set it up in the sky. The flying things tried to move it but it did not move. The Tciktcikano (a bird like a wren) tried to move it and it rose a short distance but fell back again. He said, "If another should help me I could carry it up," so Buzzard and Tciktcikano helped each other. Grasping it on each side they flew up with it. They carried it up and placed it in the sky, and when they came back the people said to Buzzard, "You shall eat animals that have died." They said to Tciktcikano, "You shall wash in cold water every morning and so you will never be sick."[81]

The stories of Rabbit's several thefts are more than just exaggerated native legends. The two stories of Rabbit's theft, one of fire and the other of the sun, mark a progression. In "Rabbit Steals Fire," fire is brought from another land for use among the people. In "Rescue of the Sun," Rabbit takes fire, in this case the sun, liberates it and makes it available for all his fellow beings. The flying creatures, wishing to raise the sun, find the task difficult. Wren, representing youth, requires help from the buzzard, an unflattering symbol of old age. Only by working together are they able to raise the sun into the sky. These stories mark a progression because fire, in Natchez belief, was both mortal and divine. The first story, "Rabbit Steals Fire," relates how Rabbit obtained the mundane fire used for light, in cooking and heating. In the second story fire is restored to its divine state, the sun. The title, "Rescue of the Sun," indicates that fire's divine nature had to be restored, that the sun had to be rescued from the earth.

What makes these Natchez legends important in our present day is their translation in human terms. The earthen pot in "Rescue of the Sun" is the interpretive key. It has a direct correlative in Natchez ceremonial preparation of the dead. Rabbit's earthen pot has a very human counterpart in the earthen funeral bier described below.

> These tombs are either within their temples, or close adjoining them, or in their neighborhood. They are raised about three feet above the earth, and rest upon four pillars, which are forked stakes fixed fast in the ground. The tomb, or rather bier, is about eight feet long, and a foot and a half broad; and after the body is placed on it, a kind of basketwork of twigs is wove around it, and covered with mud, an opening being left at the head for placing victuals that are presented to the dead person. When the body is all rotted but the bones, these are taken out of the tomb, and placed in a box of canes, which is deposited in the temple.[82]

The Rabbit stories are like footprints on a dusty road. They connect Natchez life with the present. Behind the crazy, dancing Rabbit is an eloquent image familiar as the human condition. The story does not find death within the earthen pot, but life and a rescued sun. When I would tell people in Louisiana that I had canoed from the headwaters they were incredulous. My canoe seemed totally inadequate to them. Yet canoes were the only form of river craft for thousands of years. If canoes have become inadequate they have been made so only recently, and mostly by those who claim to be taming the river. Canoes are entirely adequate river craft having no need for levees, dams, dikes, revetments, earthworks or control structures. And it is not canoes that have made the river a polluted moat. A canoe is wonderfully organic, requiring only the willful act of a paddlestroke. Repeating those paddlestrokes keeps a canoeist moving in concert with the river. Rabbit, with his head ablaze, embodies hope. Hope is rising each day at dawn to greet the sun, whether chieftain or simple, nameless, embracing the unknown and going blindly forward without resources. Hope is like one's paddlestrokes, repetitious as breathing, propelling one's small craft, one's fragile earthen pot. Hope is that most necessary cardinal virtue.

French officers cantoned amongst the Natchez coveted their lands. M. de Chopart, commandant of nearby Fort Rosalie laid claim for himself to the principal village, White Apple. He demanded payment for the crops sown there. The Natchez Suns passed out bundles of sticks, ostensibly to measure parcels of tribute. In reality the bundles were timers, each stick representing a day to wait before attacking the French. On November 28, 1729 the Natchez massacred Chopart with 700 of his countrymen. Two years later, after several battles, French troops cornered the remaining Natchez near Natchitoches. The French annihilated the Natchez, taking some four hundred captive. The women and children were shipped to Santo Domingo and sold as slaves. Most of the warriors were executed in New Orleans. Probably amongst their number was the chief, the Great Sun.

In 1976 the Grand Village of the Natchez was dedicated as a National Historic Landmark within the US Park Service. Archie Sam, one of the last surviving Natchez, spoke at the dedication ceremonies.

"Maybe we can never re-build the fires of the old days." He explained that legend teaches that the ceremonial fires were brought from heaven and were holy. "The old ones say we are too profane to light the fires."[83]

I began my river trip after having been laid off from a job of ten years. The layoff had nothing to do with work. Instead it had to do with a peace vigil that I had organized in La Crosse two days before the first Gulf War began, on Martin Luther King's birthday. Called "River on Fire", some eight hundred people prayed, lit candles and walked down to the river hoping for peace. The vigil so irritated my boss that he laid me off. So began my river trip at the headwaters, my finding of Hole-in-the-Day. As happens during an eclipse, my world then had grown suddenly and unexpectedly dark, had changed in fundamental ways. I had grasped about seeking fundamental truths, deep desires, trust, faith, some guide to follow. My desire then was peace.

Further on, after leaving home a second time, departing La Crosse, I left even more behind: car and gear, friends, work and fear of not working. And I left some of myself as well, my old self. This was the lesson of Black Hawk, and the Adventures of Injun' Joe. My view of home informed my view of the world. It had been a pretty parochial view. Sometimes our villages are destroyed because we try too hard to save them. Things aren't always as they appear.

At St. Louis there was confluence and relationship. So many things came together for me there and still do: the great hoop, peace within, the gathering of waters and strength to carry on. And moving on from there as though in a dream, entering onto the King's Highway, I learned how true leadership arises from compassion and expresses itself in service. Only right relationships endure.

The Mississippi voyage was my retreat, paddle therapy to dissolve bitterness and find a new life. Over twenty-five hundred miles on from its beginning I was still wondering if I had done the right thing. On the last day of my journey, in LaPlace, Louisiana, I went to the public library and found this.

> On Christmas Eve the "feu de joie," the fires of joy, will leap skyward to greet the Christmas season along the Mississippi in the River Parishes...In St. John Parish, those attending midnight Mass had always lit the fires to show the way to church and as beacons for those who have to cross the dark waters of the river...[84]

It's hard for a Northerner to feel Christmas spirit in mid-August in southern Louisiana. But I did. I really did. Discovering feu de joie made me feel like my dead-reckon navigation had worked just fine. It made me think my primitive journey was worth every paddlestroke. For the first time in months I felt like I really knew what I was doing.

My canoe stayed in New Orleans a long time. Arrangements for its return to La Crosse unraveled like channels in a bayou. Trusting a stranger's promise I tied the canoe crosswise onto a trailer and walked away from the river. It was August 29, three and half months since leaving Itasca, and I was broke. With no money, no wallet, no ID and no contacts in the city there weren't a lot of options. In the end New Orleans was kind to me. Lee Scott, who operates an air conditioning business near the river, staked me $20 for a room at the local YMCA. It was enough.

Next morning I collected General Delivery mail, and in it were a new credit card and bankcard. I was becoming an economic person again. I repaid Lee his $20 loan and then wandered New Orleans. Margaret would arrive the next afternoon. Toward evening, as if by habit, I went to the river. At a drugstore I bought a carton of chocolate milk, a bag of shelled pecans and a pack of cigarettes. Headed downtown I walked past Lee Circle, a roundabout pillared with a statue of the Southern general. Park benches on its perimeter were vacant but for pigeons and a gaunt black man about my age. He fixed me with the stare of a needy person, one not yet broken by poverty. I asked if he wanted something to eat. Saying nothing he smiled weakly. All of his front teeth were wired together. Then I noticed the bruises all around his face. He had been badly beaten. Palming the cigarettes, I gave him the milk and pecans. He nodded in thanks and I wondered all the way to the river how he was going to eat those nuts.

A car ferry operating from Canal Street crosses passengers for a quarter. The river is over two hundred feet deep there. I stood at the rear railing looking down from the stern watching the waters roil backwards in a phosphorescent trail. There was a disturbing sense that the river was withdrawing from me, again, as it had at Lake Itasca. But here was no enticing mosaic of glittering moon glass. Here in New Orleans the river was in turmoil, swirling away in madness, or anger, or frustration, like Van Gogh's Starry Night. Slowly I crumbled tobacco from the cigarettes' little paper cylinders into the ferry's wake. The grains were my offering, connecting me with the river and then beyond, far beyond. Though I couldn't see it happen, I knew the river was already pulling the tobacco into a single straight line. Spread the entire width of the channel as we crossed, the tobacco would nevertheless enter the sea in a long single file.

All the length of the river I'd found stories scattered like detritus from a flood. Hardly any were complete. Most were incidents and fragments, glass mosaics aswirling. It has taken some time to put them together. River names and legends, history, river art and romance, tradition, boats and trade, all are the river's face, its surface. But the real current of the river lies deeper, in the life stories of the people, us people. Often ocean-going ships would overtake me on the lower river, their size, speed and wake intimidating my little canoe. The anchor eyes with orange rust streaks running down to the water line seemed baleful and menacing. Tug-battered metal sides ribbed by inner supports heaved through the river like great, hungry leviathans. Inevitably at each ship's rear were pale, flatfaced crew quarters, the enigmatic personhood of each vessel. But almost always I could pick out some person up there. It's striking how unique the human form is. For the whole trip I could pick out people. High over the river's bluffs, working the barges, in the midst of pipes, or coils of hawser they might be standing, or fishing, working or walking. Even behind the sun-shielded windows of the pilot houses I could discern the distinctive human form. Often we would wave to one another. It's such a simple act, greeting, establishing both identity and relationship. People, we people and all our fragments of stories swirling together, are the river's deepest current. We are the road of souls.

Margaret, having a long holiday weekend, flew in from St. Louis to meet me and help celebrate my odyssey's completion. We stayed in the French Quarter, enjoying its romance as a complement to our own. Dodging intermittent showers we'd shelter in the little shops. In one we bought pecan pralines and in another chicory coffee. At Kaldi's we sat for hours on stools at the window writing postcards and watching people in the street. Outside the Café du Monde a posing mime dressed and painted all in white endured the rain without moving. We, beneath the green tent only inches away, sampled beignets. Powdered sugar from the pastries dusted our chins white as the mime's. Always there were strains of jazz suspended in the heavy air. Street musicians noodled clarinets and saxophones on busy corners. Their notes threaded the ironwork railings, tying the Quarter together like a string of Carnival beads. New Orleans for us was a very intimate place.

Saturday night Margaret and I went downtown to the river. We bought tickets for a dance cruise on the *Natchez*, New Orleans' paddlewheeler. Around midnight, after all of the other guests had gone inside, we were alone outdoors on the upper deck. Sitting side by side at the rail we watched the city passing by. All of my summer was there. For me, the lights, music, people, even the wind, were familiar. Then suddenly, everything began clearing away, like colored leaves from a tree made bare by the winter's wind. The river was drawing them to itself, retracting everything into its flowing blackness. I leaned forward in my deck chair, elbows on my knees and hands clasped together. I bent my head and closed my eyes, taking the simple tally of my soul. In my heart I could feel the river's current like my own pulse. I knew its source and end, its power. Somehow the summer's experience had contained my world and life into a simple, childlike image. Sand and water, current and craft, myself. It wasn't much to offer and yet I suspected it was more than I would ever be capable of offering again. Praying that I understood the bargain well enough, I lifted all of my senses to Margaret and asked her to marry me.

Her eyes, warm and open as incandescent amber, spoke more eloquently than my simple words. While I was yet questioning they gave the truest answer, love. She already knew my heart and what it had to say. She already knew her answer. The river, like her obedient servant, had snatched my every word away, leaving nothing between us. For a moment we were completely silent. It was as though I had never spoken. Margaret's words, when they finally came, were quiet and even. They were not a simple answer keyed to my question. She gave me not only assent, but an imperative. Her reply embraced my world. More, she showed me a glimpse of what our life together could become. "I would be honored to be your wife." Honored.

The next morning I read a newspaper over creamed and sugared coffee, something I hadn't done in months. Engrossed in an article about the Berlin Wall I hadn't noticed Margaret's approach at first. Rising from my chair I started to greet her, but she shushed me, putting her fingers to her lips. "Say 'Rabbit, Rabbit'," she whispered. Strange, I thought. Not understanding her instructions I continued to greet her and pull out a chair. "Say 'Rabbit, Rabbit'," she repeated, "It's the first of the month." As though a new month were sufficient reason, I obediently complied, "Rabbit, Rabbit." Margaret could not explain the strange invocation except on tradition from her grandmother. As a little girl she'd been told to say "Rabbit, Rabbit" first thing in the morning on the first day of every month.

It seems to me that Margaret's saying "Rabbit, Rabbit" once a month represents considerable economy. This simple dispensation is much easier and handier than rising daily at dawn to howl and wave one's arms in directing the sun across the sky as the Natchez chiefs did.

Here is the last river story. It is about the Yamasee, another Muskogean tribe of the lower river.

> The Yamasee were good people. They did not want to fight, but, being harassed, they walked deep into the water very humbly, singing pretty songs, and so that tribe was lost. The old people said that this happened because it was in the thought of God that it should be so.

I went looking for peace on the Mississippi river one summer and found these stories, this long beautiful song, this road of souls. And I found Margaret, my wife. Seems it was in the thought of God that it should be so.

Afterword

Finding George III

Margaret and I have been married since 1992 and events along the Mississippi continue to play an important role for us. In 2002 Margaret was working as curator at the Villa Louis, the historic home of an early Wisconsin fur trader. The Villa is situated on the Mississippi at Prairie du Chien, Wisconsin and is under restoration by the Wisconsin Historical Society. Through Margaret's work we learned of an Indian peace medal, minted circa 1800, found in the effects of an old bachelor who died without heir. The medal is British, bearing the likeness of King George III of England. It is a rare medal, highly prized amongst numismatists and valuable.

The deceased's name was Egidius Schoeffer III, a shoe salesman known locally as "Shady." Shady was a nickname he'd picked up at the outset of WWII when he took up farming to avoid the draft. His grandfather, Egidius I, had been a gardener, an immigrant from Bavaria. All three generations lived their entire lives in the same home. Prairie, a small, very old community on the banks of the Mississippi River sits at the confluence with the Wisconsin River. It is fitting that an old token from another empire, once so important in the events of the frontier, should lie buried there in the murky waters of obscurity for two hundred years. The story of its finding is a wonderful, complex and humbling allegory for our present efforts at peace. The medal had been issued during the reign of King George III of England. Known for a time as "Farmer George," it was George III who surrendered the colonies to become our United States. By that time George was already exhibiting signs of an incapacitating illness and later he would be called "Mad King George." In 1811 the Prince Regent, later George IV, formally assumed power. Finally, in 1820, George III died, having spent his last years in seclusion, blind as well as mad.

There were a number of treaties held at Prairie du Chien going back to French presence at Fort St. Nicholas in the 1600's. Following the French and Indian War the fort and community passed into English possession. Later still, following the Revolution, it changed hands again and became American. During the War of 1812 the British returned briefly for an encore. They captured the fort from the Americans in a battle fought in the blistering heat of high summer. It was a battle of great thirst and no fatalities. Though the Americans abandoned the fort and Prairie, the war itself was won elsewhere and the British retired.

The Villa, a Victorian-era mansion, was built by H. Louis Dousman, son of Hercules Dousman, an early Mississippi river agent of John Jacob Astor and the American Fur Company. The Villa was constructed atop the foundations of the American Fort Crawford, itself outdated by an older French Fort St. Nicholas and exactly atop a mound, most likely an Indian mound. So Villa's commanding view of the Mississippi is both a classic centering and a layering of river history as well.

Today the Villa Louis is undergoing a million-dollar restoration and is renowned for the completeness of its Dousman collection. Personal artifacts of the family were donated, including most of the home furnishings, correspondence and an excellent assortment of documentary photos. As recently as 1991 an attic trunk in a St. Paul, Minnesota home belonging to a deceased Dousman heir opened a new trove for the Villa. The trunk's contents firmly established provenance for many objects from the original estate. Among the attic documents are two photos of Egidius I. He was the Dousmans' gardener. In the earliest photo he poses with his wife for a studio portrait. In the later photo he reposes alone, in a coffin having met his end of days. But none of the Villa records mention garden tools; such humble tools apparently escaped notice.

It is against the background of the Villa restoration that Egidius Schoeffer's estate with the peace medal and his garden tools came to light. It's possible that Egidius I did his gardening amidst ruins of Fort Crawford. Mortared limestone walls of the Dousmans' garden shed lean only yards away from footings of the fort. Fort Crawford was abandoned in 1831 while the first Dousman house was begun in

1843. The Schoeffer tools are of common type. Handles on several were obviously handmade. A mattock, a grass knife and corn knife, spades and shovels, axes, hoes and scythes, a gambrel stick. All of the tools had been well maintained, their metal parts oiled against rust. It was as though they had been kept ready for use.

Peace medals are relatively small and highly portable. One can imagine plausible scenarios whereby the medal might have moved from some chieftain's breast over time to the desk drawer of a shoe salesman. Perhaps the medal was relinquished at Fort Crawford in an exchange for an American one. Such exchanges were common following the Revolution. One can imagine that the British medal was not highly prized by American officialdom. Perhaps it was lost when the fort was relocated from the flood-prone river island to higher ground. Or perhaps the medal changed hands in a game of chance, or in barter for whiskey. Frontier wives and children were traded for as much. Or perhaps the medal has always changed owners through the medium of death. Medals were often buried with their owners and garden tools would serve passably well in exhuming a body. In any case, death, in this case Egidius III's, is a wonderfully reliable transfer agent.

John W. Adams, a modern numismatist, has closely studied British peace medals. Adams identifies the series of medals of the type found in Schoeffer's estate as "Large Undated Medals of George III:76mm." They are different from preceding George III medals.

> Bewigged, the king is featured as fat-cheeked and fat-lipped. What is new is that a full suit of armour has been added, a touch that reveals a secret. Unlike the Montréal medals, which were awarded for past service (Johnson) or future identification (Amherst) and the Happy While Uniteds, which celebrated peace, these are war medals. Clearly, the designer believed the Indians would be impressed by a warlike monarch. Clearly the purpose of the production was to recruit military allies, not to celebrate passive diplomatic ties.[85]

This particular medal also displays a distinct fault that had occurred due to a crack in the medal's casting die for the obverse side. The fault line runs across the king's shoulder, upwards, toward the middle of his name, Georgius. A crack in the armour caused by a crack in the die. The distinct crack situates this medal in the George III series. In 1999 there were fifteen such pieces in known collections throughout the world. The Schoeffer discovery makes sixteen.

I had opportunity to hold the medal. It was badly discolored from oxidation and the detail on the reliefs was not clear. It is worn. Both the clasp and the relief detail are smoothed from wear. Holding the medal was like grasping a person's hand, or holding an old shoe. There was something familiar about it. I thought then how that medal might have been worn smooth by a chief such as Black Hawk. It rekindled for me all the long hours and many truths of my river journey. How ironic that the first, perhaps only, peace medal I would ever hold should bear the image of George III, Mad King George.

The rain this spring is constant. Our little creek keeps flooding and our driveway keeps washing out. We haven't been able get our garden planted. It reminds me of the floods in St. Louis in 1993 and 1994, the first years of our marriage. And in 2001 the Villa grounds at Prairie flooded, again because of heavy rains. Margaret used my canoe to paddle from building to building that spring. We'd recovered the canoe from New Orleans a couple years earlier and are very glad to have the old friend back. Maybe it was after similar flooding or after such heavy rains that Schoeffer found the peace medal. All these recent rains and flooding seem unnatural to me. Seems like we need peace with heaven itself. Perhaps we should mint a medal for the clouds.

Then had thy peace been as a river, and thy righteousness as the waves of the sea.

Index

Endnotes

[1] *Collections of the Minnesota Historical Society, Vol. V,* St. Paul, MN, 1885, p73

[2] *The Religion of the Dakotas,* James Lynd, Historical Society, St. Paul, MN, 1864

[3] *The Land Called Morrison: A History of Morrison County with Brief Sketches of Benton, Crow Wing and Todd Counties,* Harold L. Fisher, Volkmuth Print Co., St. Cloud, MN, 1972

[4] *Aitkin 1871-1971, The Centennial Story of a Town*

[5] *Lincoln's Secretary Goes West; Two Reports by John G. Nicolay on Indian Frontier Troubles, 1862,* ed. Theodore C. Blegen, Sumac Press, La Crosse, WI, 1965

[6] *Through Dakota Eyes, Narrative Accounts of the Minnesota Indian War of 1862,* ed. Gary Clayton Anderson/Alan R. Woolworth, Minnesota Historical Society Press, St. Paul, MN, 1988

[7] *Through Dakota Eyes, Narrative Accounts of the Minnesota Indian War of 1862*

[8] *Through Dakota Eyes, Narrative Accounts of the Minnesota Indian War of 1862*

[9] *AN APPEAL FOR THE RED MAN,* Bishop Whipple, 1863

[10] *Lincoln's Secretary Goes West; Two Reports by John G. Nicolay on Indian Frontier Troubles, 1862*

[11] *History of the Sioux War,* Isaac V.D. Heard, Harper & Brothers, New York, NY, 1864

[12] *Black Hawk and the Warrior's Path,* Roger L. Nichols, University of Arizona, Harlan Davidson, Inc., Arlington Heights, IL, 1990

[13] *Huck Finn and Tom Sawyer Among the Indians,* Mark Twain

[14] *The Black Hawk War 1831-1832,* vol. II, part 1, comp. and ed. Ellen M. Whitney, Illinois State Historical Library, Springfield, IL, 1973

[15] *The Black Hawk War 1831-1832*

[16] *The Owl Sacred Pack of the Fox Indians,* Truman Michelson, U.S. Govt. Printing Office, Washington, 1921

[17] *The Black Hawk War 1831-1832*

[18] *Adventures of Huckleberry Finn,* Mark Twain, 1885

[19] *The Black Hawk War 1831-1832*

[20] *The Black Hawk War 1831-1832*

[21] *Speech of Mr. Wilde of Georgia, U.S. House of Representatives, May 20th 1830,* Gales & Seaton, Washington, 1830

[22] *Adventures of Huckleberry Finn*

[23] *The Black Hawk War 1831-1832*

[24] *Adventures of Tom Sawyer,* Mark Twain, 1876

[25] *That Disgraceful Affair, The Black Hawk War,* Cecil Eby, W.W. Norton & Co., Inc., New York, NY, 1973

[26] *Adventures of Huckleberry Finn*

[27] *Life of Black Hawk,* Black Hawk, autobiography translated by Antoine Leclair, 1833

[28] *Adventures of Tom Sawyer*

[29] *Adventures of Tom Sawyer*

[30] *Huck Finn and Tom Sawyer Among the Indians,*

[31] *The Treaties of Portage des Sioux,* Robert L. Fisher, Mississippi Valley Historical Society, 1938

[32] *PrairyErth: (A Deep Map),* William Least Heat-Moon, Houghton Mifflin, Boston, 1991, pp120-1

[33] *Handbook of North American Indians,* Hodge, Government Printing Office, Washington, 1910, p89

[34] *Journal of Zebulon Pike,* Thwaites, footnote p34

[35] *War and Peace Ceremony of the Osage Indians,* Francis LaFlesche, U.S. Government Printing Office, Washington, 1939, p210

[36] *Handbook of North American Indians,* p959

[37] *19th Annual Report, Bureau of American Ethnology,* J.W. Powell, U.S. Govt. Printing Office, Washington, 1900

[38] *Jesuit Relations 1673-75,* Thwaites ed. LIX, 139, 1900

[39] *Fortieth Annual Report of the Bureau of American Ethnology, Origin of the White Buffalo Dance,* Truman Michelson, Washington, 1925, p55

[40] *The Sacred Pipe,* Black Elk, edited by Joseph Epes Brown, University of Oklahoma Press, Norman, OK, 1956

[41] *Memphis Down in Dixie,* Shields McIlwaine, E.P. Dutton & Co. Inc., NY, 1948, p43

[42] *Account of an Expedition,* comp. Edwin Long, H.C. Garey & I. Lea, Philadelphia, 1823

[43] *The Sacred Pipe,* p115

[44] *Offering Smoke, The Sacred Pipe and Native American Religion,* Jordan Paper, The University of Idaho Press, Moscow, ID, p39

[45] *War and Peace Ceremony of the Osage Indians,* pp225,250

[46] *The Sacred Pipe,* p6

[47] *The Sacred Pipe,* pxix-xx

[48] *A Drinking Song, The Collected Poems of W. B. Yeats,* Macmillan Publishing Co., Inc. NY, 1956

[49] *The Sacred Pipe,* p107

[50] *Camino Real,* Tennessee Williams, Ashley Famous Agency, Inc., New York, 1953

[51] *Camino Real*

[52] *Camino Real*

[53] *Camino Real*

[54] *Camino Real*

[55] *Camino Real*

[56] *Camino Real*

[57] *Camino Real*

[58] *Camino Real*

[59] *The Civil War: An Illustrated History,* Geoffrey C. Ward, Alfred A. Knopf, NY 1990

[60] *Camino Real*

[61] *Camino Real*

[62] *Camino Real*

[63] *Camino Real*

[64] *Camino Real*

[65] *Camino Real*

[66] *Camino Real*

[67] *Camino Real*

[68] *Camino Real*

[69] *Phillips County Historical Quarterly,* Helena, AR

[70] *Camino Real*

[71] *Fleur de Lys and Calumet, Being the Penicaut Narrative of French Adventures in Louisiana,* trans. & ed. by Richebourg Gaillard McWilliams, Louisiana State Press, Baton Rouge, LA

[72] *History of Louisiana, or the West Parts of Virginia and Carolina,* trans. by M. Le Page Du Pratz, London, T. Beckett, 1774

[73] *Mississippi as a Primitive Territory & State with Biographical Notices of Prominent Citizens,* J.F.H. Clairborne, VI, Jackson, MS, Power & Barksdale, 1880

[74] *History of Louisiana, or the West Parts of Virginia and Carolina*

[75] *Fleur de Lys and Calumet, Being the Penicaut Narrative of French Adventures in Louisiana*

[76] *Fleur de Lys and Calumet, Being the Penicaut Narrative of French Adventures in Louisiana*

[77] *Morning Advocate, November 3, 1988,* Bob Anderson, Baton Rouge, LA

[78] *Pueblo Chieftain, January 22, 1987,* Robert Walters, Newspaper Enterprise Association, Pueblo, CO

[79] *Fleur de Lys and Calumet, Being the Penicaut Narrative of French Adventures in Louisiana*

[80] *Myths and Tales of the Southeastern Indians,* John R. Swanton, US Govt. Printing Office, Bureau of American Ethnology Bulletin 88, Washington, 1929

[81] *Myths and Tales of the Southeastern Indians*

[82] *History of Louisiana, or the West Parts of Virginia and Carolina*

[83] *Natchez County Democrat,* 9-1-1976

[84] *Fires of Joy, 260-Year-Old Louisiana Celebration Ushers In Yule In Flaming Splendor,* The Times Picayune, New Orleans, LA, December 21, 1980

[85] *THE INDIAN PEACE MEDALS OF GEORGE III or His Majesty's Sometimes Allies,* John W. Adams, 1999

The Road of Souls
Reflections on the Mississippi

by Nick Lichter

Use this form to purchase additional copies directly from Wing Dam Press for $14.95 each.

Please include $3.95 shipping and handling for one book, and $1.95 for each additional book. Wisconsin residents must include applicable sales tax. Canadian orders must include payment in U.S. funds, with 7% GST added.

Payment must accompany orders. Allow 3 weeks for delivery.

Name _____

Organization _____

Address _____

City/State/Zip _____

Phone_____

Email _____

Mr. Lichter is available for speaking engagements with sufficient notice. Make inquiries at the address listed below.

Please make your check payable and return this form to:

Wing Dam Press
P.O. Box 200
Ferryville, WI 54628
www.wingdampress.com
Nlichter@wingdampress.com